EDITIONS

ARMENIAN
BULGARIAN
BURMESE (Myanmar)
CHINESE
DUTCH
ENGLISH
　Africa
　Australia
　Chinese/English
　India
　Indonesia
　Japan
　Korean/English
　Korean/English/
　　Japanese
　Myanmar
　Philippines
　Singapore
　Sri Lanka
　United Kingdom
　United States
ESTONIAN
FRENCH
GREEK
GUJARATI
HINDI
HUNGARIAN
IBAN/ENGLISH
ILOKANO
INDONESIAN
ITALIAN
JAPANESE
KANNADA/ENGLISH
KISWAHILI
KOREAN
MALAYALAM
NEPALI
NORWEGIAN
ODIA
POLISH
PORTUGUESE
　Africa
　Brazil
　Portugal
RUSSIAN
SINHALA
SPANISH
　Caribbean
　Mexico
　South America
　United States
SWEDISH
TAMIL
TELUGU
THAI
URDU
ZULU (radio)

Sarah Wilke
Publisher

INTERDENOMINATIONAL
INTERNATIONAL
INTERRACIAL

35 LANGUAGES
Multiple formats are available in some languages

The Upper Room
September–December 2014
Edited by Susan Hibbins

The Upper Room © BRF 2014
The Bible Reading Fellowship
15 The Chambers, Vineyard, Abingdon OX14 3FE
Tel: 01865 319700; Fax: 01865 319701
Email: enquiries@brf.org.uk
Website: www.brf.org.uk
BRF is a Registered Charity

ISBN 978 0 85746 044 8

Acknowledgments

The New Revised Standard Version of the Bible, Anglicised Edition, copyright © 1989, 1995 by the Division of Christian Education of the National Council of the Churches of Christ in the USA. Used by permission. All rights reserved.

The Holy Bible, New International Version (Anglicised edition) copyright © 1979, 1984, 2011 by Biblica. Used by permission of Hodder & Stoughton Publishers, an Hachette UK company. All rights reserved. 'NIV' is a registered trademark of Biblica. UK trademark number 1448790.

Extracts from the Authorised Version of the Bible (The King James Bible), the rights in which are vested in the Crown, are reproduced by permission of the Crown's Patentee, Cambridge University Press.

Scriptures quoted from the Good News Bible published by The Bible Societies/HarperCollins Publishers Ltd, UK © American Bible Society 1966, 1971, 1976, 1992, used by permission.

Extracts from CEB copyright © 2011 by Common English Bible.

Printed by Gutenberg Press, Tarxien, Malta.

The Upper Room: how to use this book

The Upper Room is ideal in helping us spend a quiet time with God each day. Each daily entry is based on a passage of scripture, and is followed by a meditation and prayer. Each person who contributes a meditation to the magazine seeks to relate their experience of God in a way that will help those who use The Upper Room every day.

Here are some guidelines to help you make best use of The Upper Room:

1. Read the passage of Scripture. It is a good idea to read it more than once, in order to have a fuller understanding of what it is about and what you can learn from it.
2. Read the meditation. How does it relate to your own experience? Can you identify with what the writer has outlined from their own experience or understanding?
3. Pray the written prayer. Think about how you can use it to relate to people you know, or situations that need your prayers today.
4. Think about the contributor who has written the meditation. Some Upper Room users include this person in their prayers for the day.
5. Meditate on the 'Thought for the Day', the 'Link2Life' and the 'Prayer Focus', perhaps using them again as the focus for prayer or direction for action.

Why is it important to have a daily quiet time? Many people will agree that it is the best way of keeping in touch every day with the God who sustains us, and who sends us out to do his will and show his love to the people we encounter each day. Meeting with God in this way reassures us of his presence with us, helps us to discern his will for us and makes us part of his worldwide family of Christian people through our prayers.

I hope that you will be encouraged as you use the magazine regularly as part of your daily devotions, and that God will richly bless you as you read his word and seek to learn more about him.

Susan Hibbins
UK Editor

In Times of/For Help with . . .

Below is a list of entries in this copy of *The Upper Room* relating to situations or emotions with which we may need help:

Addiction: Oct 29; Nov 4
Anger: Nov 17
Anxiety: Oct 14, 17; Dec 3, 5, 29
Assurance: Dec 16
Bible reading: Sept 24; Oct 5, 25; Nov 22, 26; Dec 2, 19
Celebration: Nov 2
Change: Sept 18; Oct 18; Nov 13, 23, 24; Dec 9, 21
Christian community: Sept 8, 28; Oct 4, 12, 29; Nov 2, 7, 10; Dec 10, 28
Compassion: Sept 9; Oct 11, 16; Nov 3, 6, 18
Creation/nature's beauty: Dec 27
Death/grief: Sept 17; Nov 4, 10, 18; Dec 12
Discouragement: Sept 27; Oct 2
Doubt: Oct 7; Nov 19; Dec 18
Encouragement: Sept 15, 20, 24; Oct 29; Nov 9; Dec 12
Evangelism/mission: Oct 3; Dec 4, 17, 21, 31
Family: Sept 10; Nov 1; Dec 8, 24
Fear: Sept 11; Nov 5; Dec 5, 15
Forgiveness: Sept 3, 27; Oct 6, 8, 26; Nov 30; Dec 18
Friendship: Nov 8, 16
Generosity/giving: Sept 1, 19; Oct 16 Nov 12, 29; Dec 6, 31
God's goodness/love: Sept 2, 23; Oct 9, 28; Nov 3; Dec 3, 29
God's presence: Sept 7; Oct 1, 5, 31; Nov 5, 10, 15; Dec 2, 9, 26
God's provision: Sept 5; Oct 3
Gratitude: Oct 11, 23; Nov 12; Dec 8, 27
Growth: Sept 4, 22; Nov 20, 22; Dec 7
Guidance: Sept 4; Oct 12, 18, 21, 30; Nov 5

Healing/illness: Sept 3, 15, 28; Oct 1, 19, 31; Nov 7, 27; Dec 9, 16
Hope: Sept 14, 18, 23; Oct 18; Nov 24, 27; Dec 14
Hospitality: Sept 8, 13; Oct 23; Nov 29
Job issues: Sept 29
Judging: Sept 1; Oct 26
Living our faith: Sept 9, 11, 25, 30; Oct 22, 24; Nov 1, 27, 29; Dec 1, 31
Loneliness: Nov 10
Materialism: Dec 26
Mental illness: Oct 6, 31; Dec 8, 25
Mission/outreach: Sept 1, 5; Oct. 26
New beginnings: Sept 17, 18; Oct 2, 17
Obedience: Sept 4; Oct 13; Nov 20; Dec 11
Parenting: Dec 24
Patience: Sept 9; Oct 10
Prayer: Sept 7, 10, 29; Oct 7; Nov 7, 11, 26; Dec 28
Renewal: Sept 16; Oct 27; Nov 3, 13
Repentance: Oct 8, 30; Nov 30
Salvation: Sept 17; Oct 26; Nov 4, 12; Dec 6, 25
Serving: Sept 6; Oct 4, 9, 16, 20, 24
Sin: Nov 17; Dec 20
Speaking about faith: Sept 5, 15, 30; Oct 1, 19
Social issues: Sept 1; Dec 4, 17, 21
Spiritual gifts: Sept 6; Oct 20, 22, 27; Dec 1, 10, 11
Spiritual practices: Sept 2, 12, 24; Oct 2, 5, 25; Nov 8, 28; Dec 7
Stewardship: Oct 12
Stress: Sept 10; Oct 21, 25
Tragedy: Sept 17; Nov 10, 18
Trust: Sept 11, 29; Oct 1, 7, 17; Nov 8, 11, 15; Dec 5, 15, 30

Seeking a Constant Connection

'Rejoice always, pray continually, give thanks in all circumstances; for this is God's will for you in Christ Jesus' (1 Thessalonians 5:16–18, NIV).

One of the joys of being a part of the Upper Room prayer ministry is leading prayer workshops from time to time. The intention is to help participants develop prayer practices, and I always delight in sharing stories that inspire new approaches.

At one recent gathering, I recounted the journey I had had to take to develop a new habit. For some time, I'd been frustrated with the occasional dirty coffee cup or plate that I found in our office break room. When a few gentle reminders failed to end the messiness, I realised if it bothered me that much, I would have to do the cleaning up myself. To do so with a willing spirit, though, I knew I had to incorporate prayer into the task. Resentment has turned to submission, and as I clean, I find myself praying for all the precious people (tidy and untidy!) who generate and sustain our vital ministry.

Similarly, one workshop participant told of her past frustrations with the household chores that often kept her from focusing on her prayer life. But then, she shared, she had a change of heart and began to 'sanctify' her tasks—as she described it—by praying for the family members who were benefiting from her necessary but humdrum work.

So often we think of prayer as what we do when we clasp our hands and bow our heads, but the apostle Paul urges us to 'pray without ceasing'. The workshop participant and I both were able to find ways to connect to God in even the most mundane aspects of life. Indeed, if we live our lives in a state of gratitude, we can find a connection to God in every breath we take.

Sarah Wilke
Publisher

Where the World Meets to Pray

Last year, 2013, marked the 75th anniversary of El Aposento Alto. Throughout the year we celebrated the work of the editors and distributors in Latin America whose efforts to share El Aposento Alto unite millions of people in prayer. In April 2013, we celebrated in San José, Costa Rica, my home country. We learned about the achievements in the distribution efforts of El Aposento Alto, and we heard about how the reading of the daily meditations has blessed so many lives. Hearing these experiences inspired us to worship our Lord and Saviour, Jesus Christ.

I invite you to pray for the distributors and lay people of the churches in Costa Rica and all of Latin America who, with love and commitment, continue to share the gospel of Jesus Christ through the pages of El Aposento Alto.

Blessings in Christ!

David Abarca
Managing Editor, El Aposento Alto

The Editor writes...

One of the most humbling, and inspiring, aspects of my work as editor of *The Upper Room* in the UK is to hear from people who have been helped by reading the magazine. Sometimes it is the daily discipline of reading the Bible and the words that follow which has helped them through a difficult patch, and very often it is a single meditation that has spoken directly to their situation. It has reassured them they are not alone, and that others who have been through something similar have been helped by their faith.

Many people comment that the meditation they have read 'was just right' for them: it seemed that God was speaking through the words of the person who had written them.

The Upper Room is unique in that its readers are also its writers; it would not exist without the willingness of people all over the world to share their experience of what God is doing in their lives. And it is true that the power of scripture means that it goes where it is needed most, perhaps far beyond where the writer expected or intended. Over the years I have read of lives being changed through someone picking up a copy of the magazine in a prison or a doctor's waiting room, or of someone being comforted as they approach the end of their life.

What about you? Have you had an experience of God's presence in your life that you would be willing to share? Do you remember the time when you were reading your Bible, and a new insight came to you from a familiar passage? Were you aware of God's presence with you when you kept watch by the bedside of someone who was ill? When you last spent time in prayer, or quietly watched a sunset, did you hear God speaking to you? All these situations and many more could be shared with *Upper Room* readers if you are willing to pick up a pen or open your laptop. New writers are always needed; so if you have been meaning to try, do please get in touch with me: susan.hibbins@brf.org.uk or via BRF.

I'll look forward to hearing from you!

Susan Hibbins
Editor of the UK edition

The Bible readings are selected with great care, and we urge you to include the suggested reading in your devotional time.

MONDAY 1 SEPTEMBER

Travelling, Broke, Hungry

Read Luke 6:33–38

The righteous will answer him, 'Lord, when did we see you hungry and feed you, or thirsty and give you something to drink?'
Matthew 25:37 (NIV)

One hot summer day, as we waited at a red light, we saw a young man up ahead, holding a sign that read, 'TRAVELLING, BROKE, HUNGRY'. We did not stop to help him. As we drove past, we debated whether or not we should go back. We decided to buy him some food and a soft drink. I returned with a bag of food and some money to give to him. As I approached, I could see a tattoo emblazoned across the young man's face. I imagined how this might make some people hesitant to help him. We were glad that we had stopped to help.

Throughout the Gospels, Jesus tells us to help others we meet on the highway of life, to put our faith into action. He encourages us to give and not look for anything in return, to love our neighbours as ourselves. Showing compassion for those less fortunate than ourselves is one way we reflect the presence of Jesus Christ in our lives.

Prayer: *Helping Father, help us to show gratitude for all that you've given to us by helping those in need. Amen*

Thought for the day: Acting on my faith means I will not pass by someone in need.

James C. Seymour, Jr (New York, US)

PRAYER FOCUS: TRAVELLERS

TUESDAY 2 SEPTEMBER

Dinosaur Bones

Read Joshua 4:1–9

Those who feared the Lord talked with each other, and the Lord listened and heard. A scroll of remembrance was written in his presence concerning those who feared the Lord and honoured his name.
Malachi 3:16 (NIV)

We keep a little bowl of rocks on our patio. These chunks of gravel and flint are nothing special. But to my young grandson, these rocks were dinosaur bones. And our garden was full of these treasures. So we leave the 'dinosaur bones' on our patio to remind us of that special little boy with the vivid imagination.

Israel was told to take stones from the middle of the Jordan and set them on the banks of the river as a reminder of their safe passage across the river. Like the Israelites, we can find hope and comfort in remembering God's watchful care when we face difficult circumstances.

As I remember God's faithfulness, I know that he remembers me and writes my name in a special book of remembrance (Malachi 3:16).

Prayer: *Thank you, Lord, for so many reminders of your love for us, as we pray, 'Our Father in heaven, hallowed be your name, your kingdom come, your will be done, on earth as it is in heaven. Give us today our daily bread. And forgive us our debts, as we also have forgiven our debtors. And lead us not into temptation, but deliver us from the evil one.'* Amen*

Thought for the day: Today I will remember God's mercy and faithfulness.

Thomas Buice (Tennessee, US)

PRAYER FOCUS: GRANDPARENTS SHARING THEIR TESTIMONY
* Matthew 6:9–13 (NIV)

WEDNESDAY 3 SEPTEMBER

That's Been Done!

Read Psalm 103:8–13

[Jesus] himself bore our sins in his body on the cross, so that, free from sins, we might live for righteousness.
1 Peter 2:24 (NRSV)

Years after the fact, the realisation of my failure as a mother hit me like a charging elephant. My children's father had abused them, and I—their mother—had failed adequately to protect them. Because of my negligence, my sons suffered immeasurable mental, spiritual and physical pain—pain that I could not heal.

Disconsolate, I lived in unrelenting sorrow and self-loathing. I had left my children vulnerable. How could I have done that? I felt that I did not deserve to live. But in one of my darkest moments, the Holy Spirit spoke to my heart: 'Jesus has already died for that; you should live.' And I knew it to be true. Long before I realised the extent of my sinfulness, Jesus died for all my sins, even this one. I could never make atonement, but Jesus already had.

Thankful for God's abundant grace, I began the journey toward healing. Through counselling I learned more about abuse and the way it distorts reality. I combated condemning thoughts by quoting scripture to remind myself that I am forgiven and deeply loved by God. I live—forgiven, accepted and loved.

Prayer: *Father of mercy, thank you for being more willing to forgive us than we are to forgive ourselves. In the name of Jesus, who heals our wounds. Amen*

Thought for the day: God wants us to live.

Grace Linwood-Michaels (Virginia, US)

PRAYER FOCUS: VICTIMS OF ABUSE

THURSDAY 4 SEPTEMBER

Running Away

Read Proverbs 3:1–12

Jonah ran away from the Lord and headed for Tarshish. He went down to Joppa, where he found a ship… [Then] he went aboard and sailed for Tarshish to flee from the Lord.
Jonah 1:3 (NIV)

Jonah knew what he was supposed to do. He was commissioned to go east to Nineveh, but he went to the sailing company and bought a ticket to go far away to the west. Maybe he was afraid or confused or simply unwilling to accept God's command. Perhaps he thought he knew better. God gave him the freedom to disobey and to choose his own path, but he also responded with a storm and later allowed Jonah to have an unpleasant stay in the stomach of a whale. Later Jonah argued his case with God, but eventually he went to Nineveh as originally proposed.

Like Jonah, we may resist God's leading, reasoning that something else is more appealing or more likely to be successful. Deep down we may be wilful, angry or just plain scared. God gives us the freedom to choose our own path, but he will meet us on whatever turn of the path we take and will lead us further on the good route he has for us. As our Saviour and deliverer, God responds to our decisions with more promptings to follow the purpose he has set for us and calls us to grow in faith and trust.

Prayer: *Dear God, we confess that we often ignore or reject your guidance. Forgive us and help us to trust that the things you desire for us are good. Amen*

Thought for the day: God guides us and gives us freedom to choose our way.

Rosemary Feull (Cambridgeshire, England)

PRAYER FOCUS: TO TRUST GOD'S GUIDANCE

FRIDAY 5 SEPTEMBER

When God Calls

Read Isaiah 55:6–11

'My thoughts are not your thoughts, neither are your ways my ways,' declares the Lord.
Isaiah 55:8 (NIV)

Just before I left on a mission trip to the Dominican Republic, the wife of a colleague gave me 24 copies of the Gospel of John—twelve in English and twelve in Spanish—to take with me.

Within days after our arrival, I had given away all 24 copies. But when it was time to visit a prison, one of the young missionaries, who stayed behind to guard our truck, returned his copy of the Gospel booklet to me, thinking it might be more useful in the prison.

As we spoke with the prisoners, those near me noticed the Gospel of John in Spanish that I held and asked for it. Because I only had one copy to give, I asked one of the prisoners if he would read the Gospel aloud to the other prisoners after we left. When he agreed, I gave him this last copy.

Back at home, I often think of the joy on that young missionary's face when he heard that the Gospel he gave up would be read aloud to 41 prisoners. And I think of the woman who surprised me by sending those 24 Gospel booklets in the first place. Once again I realised that when God calls us to mission, he also equips us—in surprising ways.

Prayer: *Giver of all good things, thank you for surprising us with the joy we find in serving you, and for equipping us with what we need for the journey. Amen*

Thought for the day: When God calls, he equips.

Robert J. Eckert (California, US)

PRAYER FOCUS: MISSION TEAMS

SATURDAY 6 SEPTEMBER

Broken, Scarred but Useful

Read 1 Corinthians 12:1–11
We have gifts that differ according to the grace given to us.
Romans 12:6 (NRSV)

Today I read a meditation in *The Upper Room* about a bus called 'Special' that was used to take Honduran villagers to church. Even though it had a cracked windscreen along with mechanical problems that couldn't be fixed, it was used for an important purpose.

Then I thought about some of the people that I know—people who are less than perfect. I thought of Joel, the pianist who is blind but who can stir people with his beautiful music; of the lady whom some people regard as strange but who offers her time to pray for others; and of the boy with Down's Syndrome who seems to know when someone is suffering and offers them hugs, even though his words are difficult to understand.

None of us is perfect. But just as God uses the bus called Special and people regarded as strange or disabled by human standards, he can use us for divine purposes. Cracked pots, broken buses, people with mental or physical disabilities—God calls each of us to special service in this world.

Prayer: *Lead us, O Lord, to awareness of our purpose in this life. Open our eyes to opportunities for service where we are, with whatever skills we have. Amen*

Thought for the day: Where we only see imperfection, God sees perfection.

Phyllis S. Church (Kentucky, US)

PRAYER FOCUS: PEOPLE WHO COPE WITH DISABILITY

SUNDAY 7 SEPTEMBER

A Direct Line

Read Psalm 139:7–12

Jesus said, 'Father, thank you for hearing me. I know you always hear me.'
John 11:41–42 (CEB)

Shirley, an acquaintance of mine, had been enjoying the solitude of a remote corner of a town park when she suddenly felt faint. Quickly, she reached for her mobile phone and dialled; yet she could not get a signal strong enough for the call to be completed. As her vision faded to black, she cried out, 'God, help me!'

Shirley woke up shortly afterwards in the back of an ambulance on its way to the hospital. At the moment she had lost consciousness, two emergency medical workers had arrived at the same corner of the park to eat their lunch. What some call coincidence, Shirley calls an answer to prayer.

Sometimes, we think we need to be in a specific place or to utter the proper prayers for God to hear us. But we don't need a special signal to contact him. No matter where we are, God is within reach. When we call out to him, he will hear.

Prayer: *Gracious Father, even the simplest prayer spoken in the remotest place reaches you. Thank you for this sure and wonderful gift. Amen*

Thought for the day: God always hears our call.

Monica A. Andermann (New York, US)

PRAYER FOCUS: PARAMEDICS

MONDAY 8 SEPTEMBER

Welcome a Stranger

Read Hebrews 13:1–3

I was a stranger and you welcomed me.
Matthew 25:35 (NRSV)

My wife and I are welcomers at Sunday worship and specifically look for those who are visitors. Remembering what Jesus said about welcoming strangers, we greet each visitor as we would welcome Christ. Many in our congregation make a special effort to offer hospitality to visitors. A man who visited our church several years ago and is now a member said to me: 'That first visit I had a knot of fear in my gut as I entered the front door. I kept asking myself "Will they accept me?"' He had not attended worship for many years, having left with the bitter taste of rejection because of his sexual orientation. He went on to say, 'That first Sunday was amazing. A number of people warmly greeted me with Christian love. As I left church, I felt an inner peace—as if I had come home after a long absence.'

Sometimes we who have been part of a local church for years forget how scary it can be to walk in as a stranger. We may also forget the importance God places on hospitality. Even so, it is relatively easy to greet strangers at church. The more difficult challenge is to be open and loving to people we encounter every day.

Prayer: *Dear Lord, help us to see everyone through your eyes of love and then to put our love into action. Amen*

Thought for the day: Welcoming strangers in our midst opens the door to entertaining Jesus.

Hugh Lake (Georgia, US)

PRAYER FOCUS: CHURCH WELCOMERS

TUESDAY 9 SEPTEMBER

The Golden Rule

Read Matthew 7:7–12

In everything do to others as you would have them do to you.
Matthew 7:12 (NRSV)

The voice of the assistant on the phone was heavily accented. She seemed nervous and unsure as she requested my details: name, address, credit card details. She left me on hold without warning me first. I became increasingly annoyed, and when she asked me several times to repeat the details of my order, I finally lost patience, told her to cancel my order and hung up (intending to phone back and get someone more competent to take my order). Then a thought struck me: 'Maybe she is a new immigrant, and this is her first day in her first job.' Perhaps if I had been more patient I could have given her some self-confidence and helped her learn how to do the work without being so nervous.

Then I remembered what Jesus said about what we do to one of the least of his sisters or brothers (see Matthew 25:31–40). I thought: 'What if this had been Jesus that I'd been talking to and I had behaved like that toward him?'

It was too late to make amends to the assistant, knowing it would be impossible to reach the same person on the phone again. All I could do was to ask God to forgive me for my insensitivity and pray that in the future I would remember to treat others as members of Jesus' family.

Prayer: *Loving God, help us to treat others kindly no matter what the circumstances, remembering that whatever we do for the least of your children, we do for you. Amen*

Thought for the day: Who needs my patience today?

Charles Levy (Ontario, Canada)

PRAYER FOCUS: CUSTOMER SERVICE REPRESENTATIVES

WEDNESDAY 10 SEPTEMBER

In God's Presence

Read Psalm 73:23–28
Come near to God and he will come near to you.
James 4:8 (NIV)

As my parents age, they are becoming more and more dependent on my help. I do what I can, but it is not easy since I work and have responsibilities in my own immediate family as well. Because life has become such a struggle for Mum and Dad, our every visit or phone conversation has become focused on the next list of requests they have for me. Sometimes I feel I have become merely a facilitator of all their needs. I'm happy to help as much as I can, but I miss just chatting and laughing and doing things together the way we used to.

This may be how God feels when I pray only when I have a list of requests. I know that he cares about my needs, and I often mention them in prayer. But I very seldom pray just to worship and be near him. I regret looking to God merely as a facilitator of requests. More and more I am realising that he wants more than my requests; he wants my heart.

Prayer: *Dear Lord, reignite our hearts with love for you. Remind us that our times of communion together can be not only about our needs but about spending time with you. Amen*

Thought for the day: Today I will treasure my time with God.

Julie Gilleand (Indiana, US)

PRAYER FOCUS: THOSE CARING FOR AGEING PARENTS

THURSDAY 11 SEPTEMBER

Even in Crisis

Read Psalm 46:1–11

I eagerly expect and hope that I will… have sufficient courage so that now as always Christ will be exalted in my body, whether by life or by death.
Philippians 1:20 (NIV)

One night my wife and I were returning home in high spirits after a house group meeting. We boarded a bus to take us home. Suddenly, a man with a gun forced the driver to divert from the route. At first I thought, 'He's a young man; I can take him.' But when I stood to try to overpower him I noticed that he was not alone. A gang of six armed men was on the bus. One of the men hit me on the head with the butt of a gun and I fell down.

The men moved from seat to seat as they robbed every passenger of their belongings. Those who resisted were beaten severely. Women screamed and men were terrified. No one came to our rescue.

Eventually, they stopped the bus and disappeared. We then realised that all our possessions were gone: handbags, wallets, mobile phones, laptops and other items. I turned to my wife, and to my surprise she was very calm. I asked her, 'How can you remain so composed?' She smiled and quoted Philippians 1:20 to me.

Since then I've learned that we can always find our strength and courage not in ourselves but in God.

Prayer: *Heavenly Father, help us to find our strength and courage in you only, for you care for us always. Amen*

Thought for the day: God's word helps us stand against hard times.

Geoffrey Omondi Odette (Nairobi, Kenya)

PRAYER FOCUS: PUBLIC TRANSPORT PASSENGERS

FRIDAY 12 SEPTEMBER

Faces

Read 2 Corinthians 3:17–18
For now we see only a reflection as in a mirror; then we shall see face to face. Now I know in part; then I shall know fully, even as I am fully known.
1 Corinthians 13:12 (NIV)

Faces fascinate me! There is an advert on television where a young woman meets her boyfriend off the train. She runs to a man, hugs and kisses him only to find she has got the wrong man. She has gone to the wrong opticians, according to the advert. I have often gone to an airport or train station to meet someone I know, and I am always amazed that, even in a huge crowd of people, I recognise the person I am meeting straight away.

We all have one pair of eyes, one nose and one mouth, yet we are all different. God made each one of us unique. Recently I met an old friend I had not seen for some years. She used to be much taller than I am, but now she is shorter and her body is crippled. But her face is still recognisable. God made each one of us beautiful in our own special and individual way. The face we see in the mirror is not the same as others see, because it is in reverse, but we are being made into God's likeness, and he loves us as we are.

One day we shall recognise Jesus. What glory that will be!

Prayer: *Thank you, Lord, for family and friends who are special to me. Thank you for making me ME! Amen*

Thought for the day: Each one of us is precious in God's sight.

Pat Rantisi (Shropshire, England)

PRAYER FOCUS: THE PEOPLE WHOSE FACES I SEE TODAY

SATURDAY 13 SEPTEMBER

Open Your Eyes

Read Luke 21:1–4

As Jesus looked up, he saw… a poor widow put in two very small copper coins.
Luke 21:1–2 (NIV)

I was at church one Sunday morning and greeted one of the faithful members of our congregation. Then I went through my regular routine as pastor. After worship I was shaking hands and wishing everyone a nice week when someone pointed out that the person I had greeted earlier had a big bandage on the end of her nose. Apparently she'd had some minor surgery the previous week. The strange thing is, I had spoken with this person four or five times that morning and had not noticed that bandage at all.

This made me wonder how often I really pay attention when I look at people. Do I focus on the person or on all the things I'm doing? When I look at them, do I really see?

Jesus really saw people. When he encountered someone, he saw their needs. They became his priority. His eyes even found the invisible ones whom everyone else overlooked, such as the poor widow who gave two coins. The first act of love is to open our eyes and truly see those around us. It means setting aside our own agenda for a moment, and that's not easy. But it's the only way to find out what—and whom—we're missing!

Prayer: *Dear Lord, teach us how to love like Jesus. Open our eyes, that we may see opportunities for serving others. Amen*

Thought for the day: How will God use me in the lives of people around me?

Michael Raypholtz (Ohio, US)

SUNDAY 14 SEPTEMBER

Consider the Lilies

Read John 1:1–5

Consider the lilies of the field, how they grow; they neither toil nor spin, yet I tell you, even Solomon in all his glory was not clothed like one of these.
Matthew 6:28–29 (NRSV)

A friend gave me a small clump of moonflowers, a variety of evening primrose. On many evenings, after the sun has disappeared from the horizon and a little light remains, I wait, thrilled with anticipation. Tightly closed buds look as if they would be days from opening; but as I watch, a stem begins to quiver a bit and soon the sides of the buds begin to burst open, showing little slits of yellow. In front of my eyes, the closed petals open into flowers. Sometimes one at a time, sometimes several at a time, the moonflowers open. My delight never diminishes.

Recently, my husband and I have been experiencing a difficult time, yet through it all we have been conscious of the prayers of many people and the faithfulness of God. The unfathomable reliability and dependability of God is like the brightness of those yellow flowers, opening in the darkness. Both bring a burst of joy, a sense of awe and the security of knowing that God is working in even the darkest situations of our lives.

Prayer: *Creator God, how delightful it is to discover that you bring blossoms in the night and hope to the dark times of our lives so that we are conscious of your presence and love! Amen*

Thought for the day: With God's help we can discover beauty in our darkest times.

Ruth Smith Meyer (Ontario, Canada)

PRAYER FOCUS: THOSE EXPERIENCING TRIALS

MONDAY 15 SEPTEMBER

The Bracelet of Blessing

Read 1 Corinthians 14:1–3

The Lord said to Abram, 'I will bless you, and make your name great, so that you will be a blessing.'
Genesis 12:2 (NRSV)

Working in a hospital, where I care for the sick and their families, I have many opportunities to love others and to offer them encouragement. One way I reach out to people is through a special kind of bracelet that I wear. The bracelet has ten links, with Christian symbols. When people see the bracelet and comment on how beautiful it is, I take it off and put it on their wrist as a sign of my love and concern for them. Often, in response, they voice varied concerns, including a need for prayer for themselves or someone who is sick and hurting. Some just need me to listen to them.

As I give away more and more bracelets I feel my faith growing stronger because I know God is working through me to encourage others and to give them hope. Every time I reach out to others, I feel blessed that my actions are bringing glory to God.

Prayer: *Healing God, you have blessed us all with a capacity to encourage and to love. Work through us to bring hope to your people as we use our gifts to glorify you. In the name of Jesus we pray. Amen*

Thought for the day: Today I will offer words of encouragement, kindness and love to a stranger.

D. Hodskins (Kentucky, US)

PRAYER FOCUS: HOSPITAL EMPLOYEES AND VOLUNTEERS

TUESDAY 16 SEPTEMBER

Creative Prayer

Read Psalm 119:121–136
Whatever you ask for in prayer with faith, you will receive.
Matthew 21:22 (NRSV)

Several years ago, I realised that my prayer life was in trouble. Praying was not a meaningful part of my daily routine. Many other things filled my days and nights.

I began to pray for God's help. Before long, a friend introduced me to a new way of praying through art, explaining how the use of colour could brighten a person's prayer life. I love colour, and I quickly became interested. In time, my prayer life took on new meaning. Some coloured pens and a sketchbook were all I needed.

After much thought, I decided that the best time for my new prayer life was in the early morning. I began to write with my coloured pens the names of family and friends, scribbling designs in and around them. As my pen was writing and colouring, I realised I was talking about the people and events in my life and listening to God's response.

Each page in my sketchbook became a visual reminder of my talks with God. The key words in Matthew 21:22—'prayer', 'faith', 'receive'—came to life. Talking with God through colour, I received the tools to revitalise my prayer life.

Prayer: *Loving God, thank you for your patience. Please help us to have faith in your holy word. Amen*

Thought for the day: How can I brighten my prayer life today?

Anita J. McIntosh (North Carolina, US)

PRAYER FOCUS: THOSE SEEKING A DEEPER PRAYER LIFE

WEDNESDAY 17 SEPTEMBER

The Shadow of Death

Read Romans 6:1–11

Though I walk through the valley of the shadow of death, I will fear no evil: for thou art with me.
Psalm 23:4 (KJV)

Even though I grew up outside one of Central America's most violent cities, I was never touched by the violence until Guillermo disappeared. Though shaken, I stayed calm, fully expecting my friend to be found unharmed because 'in all things God works for the good of those who love him' (Romans 8:28, NIV). So when I heard he was dead, I could not believe the news. Surely God would never let anything happen to Guillermo, the inspiring worship leader and thoughtful friend whose 20th birthday was just around the corner; Guillermo, who kept in touch with me after I moved far away; Guillermo, who noticed and told me I looked pretty the first time I ever wore make-up. Now I was putting on make-up for his funeral.

That funeral was the most powerful, beautiful event I had ever experienced. Guillermo touched so many lives by living unreservedly for God. Now, through his death, we who knew him were challenged to follow his world-changing example.

The promise in Romans 8:28 is still true. Guillermo is more alive now than he ever was on this earth, and many people are living with a new sense of purpose. At the time we did not understand, but God really was working for good.

Prayer: *All-powerful God, help us to trust you and to follow you in everything, without holding back. In Jesus' name. Amen*

Thought for the day: Even in tragedy we can trust God's promises.

Ellen M. Williamson (Indiana, US)

PRAYER FOCUS: VICTIMS OF VIOLENCE

THURSDAY 18 SEPTEMBER

Beauty in Transition

Read Ecclesiastes 3:1–8
For everything there is a season, and a time for every matter under heaven.
Ecclesiastes 3:1 (NRSV)

During late September and early October in North America, the change in seasons requires different kinds of activity. There are bulbs to plant and preparations must be made for winter. This is a transition time marked by unique beauty.

Changing seasons can be a metaphor for life itself. Life is filled with change and transitions. Perhaps these are natural processes of growing up and growing older. We welcome many changes with eager anticipation: self-discoveries, new relationships, finding a satisfying career, a new home, spiritual awakenings. But some changes are unwelcome intrusions: loss of relationships, changes in home life and personal life, work or financial setbacks, health challenges. All are a part of our normal life journey. How we handle them can make all the difference in life.

We need our transition times so that we won't get stuck in the past. We may not welcome every transition in life, but we do have a choice in how we will respond. In my experience, those who look ahead with hope to the new season are happier people and always able to find some good in every situation. We behold the unique beauty of every transition when we take the time to see how God is moving us toward a new future with meaning and purpose.

Prayer: *O God, as we undergo changes in our lives, remind us that we can rely on you day to day. Amen*

Thought for the day: God stands with us during our changing seasons of life.

F. Richard Garland (Rhode Island, US)

PRAYER FOCUS: THOSE RELUCTANTLY UNDERGOING CHANGE

FRIDAY 19 SEPTEMBER

Ministry of Fasting

Read Isaiah 58:6–12

The Lord will guide you continually, and satisfy your needs in parched places, and make your bones strong.
Isaiah 58:11 (NRSV)

As I have completed my prison term here in Florida, I have come to appreciate the spiritual discipline of fasting. It has become a ministry for me. I always ask the Holy Spirit, 'To whom should I give my meal tray today?' Many times, the Spirit shocks me by leading me to give my meal to someone who isn't a Christian. Often it's someone I don't even care for. The thought of giving my meal to someone like this at first seems like a mistake. I understand the Spirit's guidance only when I see the look on his face as I hand him the tray and say, 'God bless you.' You see, most of the men here in prison are not used to kindness. I thank God for using me to show them some.

Prayer: *Thank you, dear God, for helping us to show kindness in unexpected ways. Lead us to take care of one another as you care for us. We pray in the name of Jesus, who taught us to pray, 'Our Father which art in heaven, Hallowed be thy name. Thy kingdom come. Thy will be done in earth, as it is in heaven. Give us this day our daily bread. And forgive us our debts, as we forgive our debtors. And lead us not into temptation, but deliver us from evil: For thine is the kingdom, and the power, and the glory, for ever.'* Amen*

Thought for the day: God's Spirit is at work even within prison walls.

Lance Ek (Florida, US)

PRAYER FOCUS: THOSE IN PRISON
* Matthew 6:9–13 (KJV)

SATURDAY 20 SEPTEMBER

This Life

Read Psalm 139:13–18
I praise you, for I am fearfully and wonderfully made.
Psalm 139:14 (NRSV)

I left the shop smiling at the lovely day and the people I met. Unexpectedly, a woman I had never seen before spoke to me. She told me that she has a serious illness, and the doctors are proposing to amputate her arm. The woman cried, 'I can't live without my arm! Is that really life?'

I empathised with her and smiled inside. When I was an infant, I fell ill with polio. Now my legs are so weak that I must use crutches to walk. I think this is why the woman approached me. I asked her if she thought my life had no value.

Until that moment, I simply accepted my body as it is. I live and rejoice in my life. But I never thought that God could use my disability as a way to help others. After we had talked, the woman calmed down and I was encouraged. I realised that though I don't have a perfect body, God gave me optimism and joy. I believe my Creator wants me to use those gifts to console those who are discouraged or in despair.

Prayer: *Thank you, O Lord, for using us to bring your love to those who especially need it. Amen*

Thought for the day: Regardless how 'incomplete' we feel, we are priceless to God.

Galina Samson (Voronezh, Russia)

PRAYER FOCUS: AMPUTEES

SUNDAY 21 SEPTEMBER

Better to Build Bridges

Read Luke 6:27–31
We must always aim at those things that bring peace and that help to strengthen one another.
Romans 14:19 (GNB)

We live in a beautiful part of the world where England and Scotland meet. Here, stone walls, skilfully erected, stretch for miles across high places, marking territory and securing pastures for flocks and herds. Here too, stone bridges hump their backs to keep roads clear of the raging torrents which often rush down narrow hill streams. They too are the product of skilled craftsmen through the years, but I am reminded of an old saying: 'Better to build bridges than to build walls.'

Our walls are mostly for protection, but sadly throughout the world people and nations put up walls which say: 'This is mine! Keep out!' Sad, because the commandments to love God and love our neighbour, which are at the heart of all our believing and living, are bridge commandments. They remind us that Jesus lived and died and lives still, to be our bridge to the Father. They tell us our Christian duty is to be open and welcoming to all—to be peacemakers. Sometimes we may find ourselves challenged to take down the cosy protecting walls of our Christian life and use the love-stones to make bridges for others to reach God.

Prayer: *Lord Jesus, you are my bridge to the Father and my bridge to a needy world. Help me to keep crossing over both of them. Amen*

Thought for the day: Walls sometimes say, 'Keep out!' Bridges mostly say, 'Welcome!'

Colin Harbach (Cumbria, England)

PRAYER FOCUS: THOSE BUILDING BRIDGES BETWEEN COMMUNITIES

MONDAY 22 SEPTEMBER

The Geranium

Read John 15:1–7
The free gift of God is eternal life in Christ Jesus our Lord.
Romans 6:23 (NRSV)

Some months ago I was given a geranium plant with four large red-orange flower clusters. In time they faded away. For weeks I had only a plant with green leaves. I was disappointed because there were no blossoms. Then I decided to add some plant food to the water. Soon I saw a short stem with buds; a few days later, I saw two more. In a few weeks there were ten clusters of buds on six-inch-long stems. What a glorious display when all the buds were fully developed.

Then it occurred to me that our lives can be like that. When we follow Jesus' teachings and practise them, we absorb qualities that provide an added dimension to life. This is God's gift to us for a life more abundant and fulfilling than we could ever imagine.

Prayer: *Thank you, O God, for revealing your very self to us in Jesus. What an awesome gift that, through Jesus, we find the road that leads us to you, and lives which are fulfilled. In Jesus' name we pray. Amen*

Thought for the day: We are made in the likeness of God with a potential for inner, spiritual growth.

Margaret Tansley (Ontario, Canada)

PRAYER FOCUS: THOSE WHO HAVE NO KNOWLEDGE OF THE BIBLE

TUESDAY 23 SEPTEMBER

Christ's Suffering

Read Isaiah 53:3–9

He was despised and rejected by mankind, a man of suffering, and familiar with pain.
Isaiah 53:3 (NIV)

Albert looked helpless as he lay on the hospital bed. A formerly energetic 50-year-old business owner and community leader, he now faced one of the most difficult challenges of his life. One year earlier, Albert's doctors had told him that he had incurable cancer. He underwent a series of treatments that often left him feeling weak and unable to work. In spite of great suffering and financial loss, he never complained. In fact, each time I visited him, he managed to smile as he spoke of God's goodness and grace.

We may never experience an illness as serious as Albert's, but all of us encounter difficult situations at some point. Albert's example showed me that, as Christians, we can find comfort in knowing that Christ understands our suffering, because he endured humiliation, persecution and pain during his time on Earth.

Today, Christ shares our pain and suffering and invites us to rest safely in his arms.

Prayer: *Dear Father, strengthen and comfort us during our times of suffering. In Jesus' name we pray. Amen*

Thought for the day: God comforts us in our suffering.

James C. Hendrix (Indiana, US)

PRAYER FOCUS: PEOPLE WITH INCURABLE DISEASES

WEDNESDAY 24 SEPTEMBER

Comfort Journal

Read Psalm 16:5–8

Praise be to the… Father of compassion and the God of all comfort, who comforts us in all our troubles, so that we can comfort those in any trouble with the comfort we ourselves receive from God.
2 Corinthians 1:3–4 (NIV)

Toward the end of her life, my grandmother went into a nursing home. I wanted to lift her spirits by finding a comforting Bible verse to send her each week. She was an amazing woman of faith, so I knew she would enjoy reading the verses. I was new to the Bible. I learned a lot as I searched for the right verses to encourage her. Many of the uplifting verses I found were in Psalms (18:2; 46:1; 62:8); but I also looked for verses she would not know so well, such as Habakkuk 3:18–19 and Zephaniah 3:17. I wrote the verses in a notebook so that I wouldn't accidentally send the same verse twice. I compiled a list of 150 verses before my grandmother died.

Afterwards, I bought a small journal, wrote the verses in it (one verse per page), and gave it to my mum, who suffers from depression. I also made journals for my mother-in-law, sister and grandson. Then my sister made one for me, which I carry in my handbag. I pull out my journal when I want a new verse to memorise or need a pick-me-up. Through these journals, my family members have shared God's comfort with one another.

Prayer: *Merciful God, help us turn toward your word for comfort and direction. Amen*

Thought for the day: Who could I help by sharing a favourite Bible verse?

Camille Evans (Florida, US)

PRAYER FOCUS: NURSING HOME RESIDENTS

THURSDAY 25 SEPTEMBER

The Light of the Cross

Read 2 Corinthians 3:12–18
You are the light of the world.
Matthew 5:14 (NIV)

It is wonderful to me that God communicates with us in many different ways. We can hear his voice in the words of scripture or a sermon. We can hear God in the words of a song, the melodies of music, or even in the sounds of nature. Sometimes, however, he gets through to us without any words at all. That's what happened to me at our last Easter sunrise service.

For that service, our church sets up seats and an altar outside in front of our cemetery. From the seats, we can see our church building in the background. Then, if it is a clear morning, and the timing is right, we can see the sun rising over the cemetery during worship. This experience by itself gives a powerful message to us about Jesus' resurrection. But last Easter, something even more powerful happened.

As the sun rose that morning, the rays hit the cross on the altar, and then reflected an image of the cross on our pastor's robe. God spoke through that image, giving me a message without words. We are all invited to reflect the glory of Christ to others. We are not the source of that divine light; but if we are in the right place and allow God to use us, others can see Christ through us.

Prayer: *Lord Jesus, help us in all that we do to reflect your glory and your love. Help us to let others get a glimpse of you when they interact with us. Amen*

Thought for the day: How do I reflect the love of Jesus to others?

David E. Spivey Jr (North Carolina, US)

FRIDAY 26 SEPTEMBER

The Supreme Architect

Read Matthew 7:24–27

Unless it is the Lord who builds the house, the builders' work is pointless.
Psalm 127:1 (CEB)

I have been an architect for over 50 years. When designing a home for a client, an architect considers the big picture: a client's needs and lifestyle, as well as aesthetics, climate, topography, durability, cost and a host of other issues. Enthusiastic clients often approach me with glossy magazines in hand, and tell me they know 'exactly what they want'; my function is simply to 'put it on paper'. If the magazine displays, for example, a luxury home on a level site, while the client, on a tight budget, wishes to build on the vineyard slopes of Cape Town, I consider the big picture and refuse the job. Wiser clients ask if we can work as a team to interpret their dreams and needs. Then, the results often exceed their expectations.

We are part of the team, all members of the body of Christ; but so often we approach God in prayer, knowing exactly what we want and enthusiastically pursuing our own dreams, desires and plans. When we work with God to interpret our dreams and needs the results will exceed our expectations.

Prayer: *Dear God, grant us the vision to fulfil our dreams in ways that honour you and bring glory to your kingdom. Amen*

Thought for the day: God's dreams for us exceed our best expectations.

Keith Honeyman (Western Cape, South Africa)

PRAYER FOCUS: ARCHITECTS

SATURDAY 27 SEPTEMBER

Broken but Forgiven

Read Colossians 1:9–14

[God has] brought us into the kingdom of the Son he loves, in whom we have redemption, the forgiveness of sins.
Colossians 1:13–14 (NIV)

One summer, my husband and I arrived home from a few days away to find large cracks in a window of our flat. We learned that while playing with friends in the nearby courtyard, a young neighbour had kicked a ball that broke the window.

The boy was usually playing outside with other children, but now he was nowhere to be seen. We went to his home, where he hesitantly came to the door, eyes downcast and shoulders slumped.

'We heard about the ball. It was an accident; it could happen to anybody,' we said. 'We forgive you.' The boy straightened. His eyes came up to meet ours, and he smiled.

When we make mistakes it's easy to wrestle with shame and withdraw from our world. We may feel that we don't deserve to be loved by God or anyone else. We sometimes have the sense that our faults are so big, they can't be forgiven.

But God sent Jesus Christ to die for us and redeem us. This grace covers us. We can hold our heads up high and meet the future with confidence, with the certainty that even in our brokenness, God forgives us.

Prayer: *Dear God, when we are feeling discouraged about our shortcomings and doubts, thank you for believing in us. Amen*

Thought for the day: God's mercy precedes our mistakes.

Lynn Hare (Oregon, US)

PRAYER FOCUS: THOSE WHO STRUGGLE WITH SHAME

SUNDAY 28 SEPTEMBER

The Prayer Blanket

Read 1 Thessalonians 5:12–24

Pray without ceasing.
1 Thessalonians 5:17 (NRSV)

While repairing my house, I slid off the roof, caught my foot in the ladder and hit the patio decking. I did not know if I had broken any bones, but I knew I was hurt. Ginger, my wife of 50 years, heard the thud and came running. I later learned that I had torn a tendon in my foot.

Before I had surgery, members of my church made a prayer blanket for me. When church members, friends and family prayed for me, they tied a knot along the edge of the prayer blanket. I took my prayer blanket to the hospital and asked my medical team to tie a prayer knot in my blanket. Some tied a braided knot. My surgeon tied a surgeon's knot, used to tie stitches. Most people tied a granny knot. Some prayed for me aloud; others closed their eyes and prayed silently. A woman from El Salvador prayed in Spanish and cried as she prayed. Their prayers were uplifting. I could feel the spirit of the Lord moving with each tied knot. Sometimes, when I was feeling a lot of pain, I held the knots in the blanket, knowing that each knot represented someone's prayer for me. My recovery will take nine months. During that time, I will continue to pray for those who prayed for me, counting each knot as I do.

Prayer: *Dear God, give us the courage and desire to pray for others. Teach us to 'pray without ceasing'. Amen*

Thought for the day: Praying for others is a blessing.

Tom Gregg (Texas, US)

PRAYER FOCUS: THOSE RECOVERING FROM SURGERY

MONDAY 29 SEPTEMBER

Something Beautiful

Read Psalm 32:1–11

I will instruct you and teach you the way you should go; I will counsel you with my eye upon you.
Psalm 32:8 (NRSV)

Our family had been packing with excitement for our move into the new house. Then, unexpectedly, my job was terminated two days after our mortgage was approved. Uncertainty loomed all around us. We had two children at college and an increased mortgage to pay. I did not know where to turn for help, so we all sat down and prayed. That time together brought us closer to one another. After that, our love for the Lord and for each other became stronger day by day. When I had been unemployed for over two months, God opened new opportunities that I had never imagined before.

Now I am working at a place where I am able to witness for the Lord more than before. We would not swap our experience during this difficult time for anything else. When we do not understand how God is working in our lives, we can pray and trust that he can work bad things for good. God can make something beautiful out of a difficult situation.

Prayer: *Faithful God, help us to understand that you are working for good even when we face challenges. In Jesus' name we pray. Amen*

Thought for the day: Challenging times can strengthen our trust in God.

Mathew Philip (Georgia, US)

PRAYER FOCUS: THOSE WHO ARE UNEMPLOYED

TUESDAY 30 SEPTEMBER

The Clandestine Christian

Read John 19:39–42

Jesus said, 'I tell you, whoever publicly acknowledges me before others, the Son of Man will also acknowledge before the angels of God.'
Luke 12:8 (NIV)

Before Jesus' death, Nicodemus was a clandestine follower of Jesus. As a member of the Jewish council, he held great political influence. Perhaps because Nicodemus feared a loss of position and power if others were to learn about his devotion to Jesus, he communicated with Jesus only under the cover of darkness.

Surprisingly, after Jesus' death, Nicodemus brought close to 100 pounds of spices to the tomb to help Joseph of Arimathea prepare Jesus' body for burial. Such a large amount of myrrh and aloes would be difficult to conceal, but at that point Nicodemus seemed unafraid that his connection to Jesus might become known. Why, after Jesus had died, would a man of Nicodemus' standing risk his reputation and job security? I think Nicodemus was emboldened because he believed that Jesus was the Messiah.

Like Nicodemus, I sometimes find myself reluctant to proclaim my belief in the Lord, worrying what people will think. I pray that God will give me the courage to live out my faith boldly. After all, Jesus gave up his earthly life when he died on the cross for me.

Prayer: *God of encouragement, give us the boldness to proclaim your sacrifice, that others might learn of your love. Amen*

Thought for the day: In what ways can I show others my devotion to Christ today?

Tammy Kennington (Colorado, US)

PRAYER FOCUS: TO REMAIN STEADFAST IN FAITH

WEDNESDAY 1 OCTOBER

Strength in Weakness

Read 2 Corinthians 12:6–10

[The Lord] said to [Paul], 'My grace is sufficient for you, for my power is made perfect in weakness.'
2 Corinthians 12:9 (NIV)

'But it is better this way.' I was surprised to hear those words from my friend Abe, who had just been diagnosed with a disease that could be fatal. At first, he had been devastated to hear that diagnosis. But after he had struggled with it and put his life in God's hands, he was able to say, 'But it is better this way.' Though my friend was not glad about his illness, he was grateful to be reminded daily how fragile life is and that he is constantly in need of God's grace and care.

The apostle Paul expresses similar thoughts about his 'thorn in the flesh'. Whatever the thorn was, he had considered it a hindrance to him in his work for the Lord and had prayed for God to remove it. But the Lord's response was, 'My grace is sufficient for you, for my power is made perfect in weakness.' Paul eventually came to realise that, in some ways, 'It is better this way.' God's power is manifested more fully when we recognise our weakness and dependence.

It has been about 45 years since my friend Abe shared the sobering news about his illness. This year Abe turned 90, sustained all these years—physically and spiritually—by the grace and love of God.

Prayer: *Thank you, Lord, for the many times when our human weakness has revealed your strength in our lives. Amen*

Thought for the day: God's grace and power shine in the darkness.

Verner Friesen (Saskatchewan, Canada)

PRAYER FOCUS: THOSE SUFFERING WITH LIFE-THREATENING ILLNESSES

THURSDAY 2 OCTOBER

Forgetting the Past

Read Philippians 3:1–15
The Lord says, 'Forget the former things; do not dwell on the past.'
Isaiah 43:18 (NIV)

As I grow older, I find that past failures sometimes dominate my memories, haunting me. How do I get past those moments when I made poor career decisions that affected my future or when I spoke without thinking and hurt other people?

Thoughts like these are paralysing. They could have been for the apostle Paul, too. He certainly had much to want to forget. Thinking he was pleasing God, he murdered Christians. When he was finally on the side of Jesus, he was rejected, beaten and stoned for his testimony. However, Paul's God-inspired philosophy gave him renewed strength and drive for the mission that became his life: 'Forgetting those things which are behind… I press toward the mark for the prize of the high calling of God in Christ Jesus' (KJV).

That has become my motto now. When negative memories attack, I remember this verse. It is as if the Holy Spirit whispers to me, 'Forget those things which are behind.' I am free to become productive once more.

Prayer: *God of grace, cleanse our minds of past mistakes that could hinder our Christian walk and work. Amen*

Thought for the day: Today I will let go of past mistakes and follow God's leading.

Elizabeth Rosian (Pennsylvania, US)

PRAYER FOCUS: THOSE HOLDING ON TO PAST MISTAKES

FRIDAY 3 OCTOBER

Knowing God

Read Ephesians 5:19–20

[Speak] to one another with psalms, hymns, and songs from the Spirit.
Ephesians 5:19 (NIV)

I wasn't brought up in the church and didn't come to know Jesus as my Saviour until I was in my early 20s. But looking back, I see that I was not without religious instruction; it just wasn't the kind that other children got at church.

God drew me near every Sunday morning as my siblings and I sat down to my mother's big breakfast. Folk singers sang to me from the pulpit of our record player. The acoustic guitars strummed a steady beat as lively, harmonic voices sang with passion about righteous living, sinful deeds and life after death.

I remember singing these songs with exuberance and joy between bites and sips at breakfast. With tapping toes and a big smile, I was praising and worshipping God—and I didn't even know it!

But I have no doubt that through my love of music I came to know God. Often we learn about God through the things we enjoy. Whether we enjoy woodworking or baking, art or opera, butterfly or coin collections, we can look at the things we love to do in new ways and discover what God is showing us through the passions of our hearts.

Prayer: *Loving God, give us wisdom and insight into how our natural passions reflect your design for knowing and serving you. Amen*

Thought for the day: How do my interests draw me nearer to God?

Miyoko E. Hikiji (Iowa, US)

PRAYER FOCUS: MUSICIANS, WRITERS AND ARTISTS

SATURDAY 4 OCTOBER

A Committee of One

Read Isaiah 6:1–10

I heard the voice of the Lord saying, 'Whom shall I send, and who will go for us?' And I said, 'Here am I; send me!'
Isaiah 6:8 (NRSV)

During the 75th anniversary celebrations of a Boys' Brigade company, several members and ex-members expressed disappointment that a reunion dinner had not been arranged. Douglas, one of the serving officers, said nothing at the time, but early the following year, he approached me to say that just such an event had been organised. I was pleased and asked Douglas to pass on my thanks to the members of the organising committee.

'Oh,' he said, 'I am the committee. I felt that something should be done, so I did it.'

Too often when we become aware of a specific need we say, 'Something should be done about it', but we do nothing ourselves. Realising that our service is needed is often God's way of calling us to act in ways that will benefit others in Jesus' name.

Prayer: *Thank you, Lord, for calling us to serve others. Help us to recognise your call and to respond, serving you in ways that benefit others. Amen*

Thought for the day: Am I willing to take the lead in serving God today?

William Findlay (Glasgow, Scotland)

PRAYER FOCUS: THOSE WHO WORK WITH YOUNG PEOPLE

SUNDAY 5 OCTOBER

Time to Sip

Read Psalm 63:1–8

O God, you are my God, I seek you, my soul thirsts for you; my flesh faints for you, as in a dry and weary land where there is no water.
Psalm 63:1 (NRSV)

This morning, a friend told me that she had attended a presentation by a famous Bible teacher. She said she enjoyed it, but she wants to go back to her Bible soon and to dig deeper into the passages that were covered, allowing more time for the truth to soak in. Her weekend experience reminded her of a marathon runner, who grabs a cup of water, gulps it down and tosses the cup away. She asked me to pray that she would soon find time to sit and sip.

I love my friend's metaphor. I need time with God as much as I need water. Like my friend, I am better off grabbing a few minutes here and there and attending an occasional group study experience than I am doing nothing at all. These opportunities keep me functioning when I am on the run just as gulps of water keep the marathon runner from collapsing. But when a race is over, runners sit down to big meals and lots of fluid to give their bodies fuel for recovery. The race that is our lives will not be over until we die, so my friend and I must find time to pause and drink in God's presence.

Prayer: *Dear God, thank you for always being available to us. Please help us consistently to make time to soak in your love and truth. Amen*

Thought for the day: We run our best race when we take time to be with God.

Jennifer Aaron (Washington, US)

PRAYER FOCUS: RUNNERS

MONDAY 6 OCTOBER

God's Word Speaks to Us Today

Read Leviticus 23:1–27
The Lord spoke to Moses, saying: Now the tenth day of this seventh month is the day of atonement.
Leviticus 23:26–27 (NRSV)

It was 4 am, dark and silent. I sat on the edge of my bed, head in my hands, sunk in the grip of a terrible depression. The last thing I wanted to do was read my Bible, but for 25 years I had kept a practice of early morning quiet times. It was not a habit easily broken.

As I came to the end of Leviticus 23, I couldn't for the life of me remember anything that I had read, except that chapter 23 had something to do with feasts.

I was about to close the Bible, but I felt compelled to at least reread chapter 23 to see what feasts the Lord had ordained for the people so long ago. In that second reading the Holy Spirit spoke to and soothed my wounded heart. As I read about the Passover offering in 23:5 and the day of atonement in 23:27, I thought about how Christ's sacrifice is like that Passover offering and that through his sacrifice, Jesus Christ atoned for my sin.

Through this reading, the glory of what God had done for me through Christ Jesus my Saviour drove away the darkness of my depression that morning with the light of the wonder of forgiveness, love, mercy and grace.

Prayer: *Steadfast and loving God, thank you for being there when we need you most. Amen*

Thought for the day: God's word delivers grace and healing.

Don Haddleton (New South Wales, Australia)

PRAYER FOCUS: THANKSGIVING FOR GOD'S MERCY

TUESDAY 7 OCTOBER

By Faith, Not By Sight

Read John 20:24–29

God is our God for ever and ever; he will be our guide even to the end.
Psalm 48:14 (NIV)

Like 'doubting' Thomas in the John 20:24–29 passage above, my faith often falls short when I cannot see answers to prayer immediately. However, I learned what real faith looks like from a woman who lost her vision. She attended a school for the blind to learn skills to function in life. In one exercise, they took the students white-water rafting. They rode small, inflatable boats down a river through wildly churning water around boulders and over rocks. I imagined how frightening that would be—loud, roaring, the boat rocking and water splashing, without being able to see what was coming next.

I asked her how she could do something that many people with full vision would be afraid to do. 'I trusted the guide,' she told me. 'I listened to what he said, paddled when he told me to, and jumped into the middle of the raft when he said "Jump!" I believed he knew where we were going and that he would get us through.'

She knew where she wanted to go, believed her guide and trusted completely in his instruction. In the same way, Jesus asks us to live not only by what we see but also by what God's word tells us and what the Holy Spirit whispers in our hearts. We know there are situations ahead that may trouble us, but God will guide us through.

Prayer: *O God, give us eyes of faith to trust you. Remind us that you see the future clearly even when we don't. Amen*

Thought for the day: Though we cannot see the future, God can guide our path.

James H. Ball (Maryland, US)

PRAYER FOCUS: WHITE-WATER RAFTING GUIDES

WEDNESDAY 8 OCTOBER

A Clean Heart

Read Psalm 51:1–12
Create in me a clean heart, O God, and put a new and right spirit within me.
Psalm 51:10 (NRSV)

As I woke up one morning and put on my glasses, I noticed they were quite dirty. The dirt had come from all the work I had done the day before: gardening and household cleaning. At the time the dirty film was building up on my glasses, I was not aware of it. Only now, twelve hours later, did I see it.

As I cleaned the glasses, I realised that this was a good reminder of the dirt of sin that we pick up throughout our lives day by day—by what we do or fail to do. Sometimes we do not realise our sin until we see it from a fresh perspective. Psalm 51 is a good example. King David has become aware, through the prophet Nathan, that he has sinned and needs forgiveness. Only God would be able to give David a 'clean heart'.

I give thanks to God that, through Christ, we will be presented to him one day as people 'without stain or wrinkle or any other blemish, but holy and blameless' (Ephesians 5:27, NIV). Even though we sin and stumble, when we ask, God will clean us up every time!

Prayer: *Dear Father God, we thank you that you clean us up, so that the sin in our lives does not prevent us from living a life that pleases you. Amen*

Thought for the day: When we acknowledge our sin and repent, God will make us clean.

Mark A. Wallace (Suffolk, England)

PRAYER FOCUS: THOSE WHO NEED A FRESH PERSPECTIVE

THURSDAY 9 OCTOBER

The Right Thing

Read Romans 12:9–13

Let each of you look not to your own interests, but to the interests of others.
Philippians 2:4 (NRSV)

Her face was sad and worried. She entered the waiting room hesitantly. She questioned a man standing nearby to be sure we were all waiting for the train she needed. She said, 'This is the first time I have done this.' She proceeded to tell a stranger that her husband had died recently.

Train staff and fellow travellers helped her get on the train, find a seat and store her luggage. As the trip ended and we got off the train, the young man who had been sitting next to her said that he thought our train had come to the end of the platform and she might have a long walk. As they passed by me, I suggested that she might be able to get help. He told me that he had her bag. I thanked him for helping her. He responded, 'It's the right thing to do.'

We are all travellers on life's journey, and God watches over us. We know the commandment to love one another, and we can choose how to respond to people who need our help. May we always show God's love to everyone we meet. It's the right thing to do.

Prayer: *Dear God, help us to notice the needs of people around us. Guide us to see what needs to be done, and give us the courage to do it. In Jesus' name, we pray. Amen*

Thought for the day: Loving one another is the right thing to do.

Mary Etta Gardner (Illinois, US)

PRAYER FOCUS: THOSE TRAVELLING ALONE

FRIDAY 10 OCTOBER

Under Watchful Eyes

Read Luke 12:22–31

Trust in the Lord with all your heart and lean not on your own understanding; in all your ways submit to him, and he will make your paths straight.
Proverbs 3:5–6 (NIV)

Last year I was trying to pursue my postgraduate degree in social work. After failing twice to qualify for our country's best social-work college, I applied to another well-known college. I easily cleared the first-round written test and group discussion. The second-round interview was crucial for admission, and I thought I performed reasonably well. However, when the results were posted, I found my name on the waiting list and not among the list of qualifiers.

My chances for admission were very slim. But having great trust and confidence in God, I was waiting for a miracle. It did not happen and I returned home feeling dejected and heartbroken.

A few days later I got a phone call from the same institution, informing me that a place had been vacated and I would be admitted to the college. I could not believe what was happening.

Today I am in my third term. This experience taught me that we are always under God's loving and watchful eyes. I've learned on a personal level to trust God, have patience and remember that he is working for our good.

Prayer: *Almighty God, thank you for being with us when we need you the most. In Jesus' name we pray. Amen*

Thought for the day: God can turn obstacles into opportunities of grace.

Sangeeta Saren (West Bengal, India)

PRAYER FOCUS: STUDENTS STRUGGLING AT SCHOOL

SATURDAY 11 OCTOBER

Send out Compassion

Read Colossians 3:12–17
Send out your bread upon the waters, for after many days you will get it back.
Ecclesiastes 11:1 (NRSV)

Once, when I was a child, I was not picked last for a team; I wasn't picked at all. The team captain who was supposed to choose the last remaining player declined to choose me. It hurt. Really hurt. But Cheryl, a girl on the other team, said, 'Come on, Jennifer. You can be on our team.'

Twenty years later, I walked into a restaurant, and there was Cheryl. Throughout the years I had thought of her and what she did for me that day. She included me. She said I was good enough. I was so choked up with emotion that I could barely speak. I thanked her for being nice to me when we were at school. Even though she remembered my face, she didn't remember my name or that day on the playground. That was OK. I did remember, and her compassion still meant a lot to me.

Ecclesiastes suggests that compassion may be returned to us. Even small acts of kindness can make a big difference in someone else's life. Our compassion is the bread we send out, and maybe one day those who enjoyed that bread long ago will be able to come back and tell us that what we did made a difference. Our acts of kindness help to bring God's love to others.

Prayer: *Dear God, help us to be kind in whatever we do and to notice when someone needs our help. Amen*

Thought for the day: Be kind and compassionate to one another (Ephesians 4:32, NIV).

Jennifer A. Johnson (Kentucky, US)

PRAYER FOCUS: PEOPLE WHO FEEL EXCLUDED

SUNDAY 12 OCTOBER

The Temple of God

Read Romans 8:1–17

Do you not know that you are God's temple and that God's spirit dwells in you? If anyone destroys God's temple, God will destroy that person. For God's temple is holy, and you are that temple.
1 Corinthians 3:16–17 (NRSV)

Years ago, when I was a theological college student serving a church, I was approached by a 15-year-old boy who belonged to another congregation. He wanted to know if it was all right to smoke. I asked him, 'What does your minister say?' He answered, 'That's just it. He tells me not to smoke but doesn't give me a reason.' We talked about how scripture proclaims that we are God's temple and that he would have to decide whether or not he would be destroying God's temple by smoking. Two weeks later he came to tell me that he had decided not to smoke.

Each day we are faced with decisions regarding our relationship to God. These decisions may not be a physical issue such as smoking. They may relate to our Christian stewardship, our relationship to others or issues at work. The decisions we make determine whether we are building or destroying God's temple. 'What would Jesus do?' is a question for each of us to ask as we determine whether our decisions will destroy or honour God's temple.

Prayer: *Dear God of mercy, give us guidance as we make decisions. Amen*

Thought for the day: We support—or destroy—God's temple by our daily decisions.

John Clendenien (Pennsylvania, US)

PRAYER FOCUS: YOUNG PEOPLE LEARNING TO MAKE DECISIONS

MONDAY 13 OCTOBER

Start Again

Read Jonah 1:1–17

Jonah obeyed the word of the Lord and went to Nineveh.
Jonah 3:3 (NIV)

A hand-held electronic game I like to play uses voice commands. By following the commands to take certain actions, a player improves and advances in the game.

Playing this game reminds me of life. In the game, players rely on the voice commands telling us what to do. And in life, if we want to be faithful, we rely on God to tell us what to do. In the game, as in life, following the commands isn't always easy.

And the game reminds me of life in another way. When you make a mistake in the game, you can always start again. Likewise, in life when we make a mistake we can always ask God for forgiveness and start over again.

It probably wasn't easy for Jonah to disrupt his life and go to Nineveh to tell others about God. It may not be easy for us to follow God's commands either. But if we listen to God and try to do what God says, we will have an everlasting life.

Prayer: *Dear Lord, please help us follow your commands, even when it is not easy. As Jesus taught us, we pray, 'Father, hallowed be your name, your kingdom come. Give us each day our daily bread. Forgive us our sins, for we also forgive everyone who sins against us. And lead us not into temptation.'* Amen*

Thought for the day: God lets us start again when we make mistakes.

Erin Matheny (Indiana, US)

PRAYER FOCUS: PEOPLE TRYING TO FOLLOW GOD'S COMMANDS
* Luke 11:2–4 (NIV)

TUESDAY 14 OCTOBER

Returning to My Egypt

Read Exodus 3:7–15
God said [to Moses], 'I will be with you.'
Exodus 3:12 (NIV)

'Here I am again,' I thought, as I drove through my home town. It was the fourth time in a month that I had found myself driving down familiar streets to help my grandmother. She had hurt herself and needed my assistance. I wanted to help her, but going back there brought up old memories that I would rather not relive. I even prayed, 'Lord, must I keep going back there? It's just too painful!'

A few weeks later the Lord turned my attention to Exodus 3:7–15. Moses had killed a man in his home town in Egypt. He fled to live in another country where, several years later, he encountered God in a burning bush. God sent him back to Egypt to lead his people, the Israelites, out of slavery. Moses did not want to go and said to God, 'Who am I that I should go to Pharaoh?' And God told him, 'I will be with you.'

Those five words sank deeply into my spirit: 'I will be with you.' This assured me that God would be with me and give me the strength I needed to persevere. With God's help, I could get through the pain and return to my 'Egypt'.

Prayer: *Faithful God, thank you for being forever by our side in times of trouble. Give us wisdom to ask for your help and courage to follow your direction. Amen*

Thought for the day: The Lord will be with us when we face difficult times.

Cindy Ryan (New York, US)

PRAYER FOCUS: SOMEONE DEALING WITH PAINFUL MEMORIES

WEDNESDAY 15 OCTOBER

Down to Earth

Read Luke 22:14–20

My tongue will talk all about your righteousness; it will talk about your praise all day long.
Psalm 35:28 (CEB)

In the quiet of the sanctuary, I heard two voices. The first said, 'I'm going to the market to get a slice of cooked meat and a few new potatoes and peas for my dinner.' The second said, 'Take, eat: This is my body, which is given for you.'

The elderly woman behind me had talked right through the Communion service, and I was irritated. This was a holy moment, not the time to be talking about our next meal.

On later reflection, I thought of hungry people, whose next meal was always at the forefront of their minds. I thought about the disciples at the Last Supper. Perhaps when Jesus broke the bread, one of them turned to his neighbour and whispered, 'I wonder if we bought enough bread?'

I thought of Jesus—God in our everyday world, uniting heaven and earth, sacred and secular—and I wondered if we sometimes make worship an escape from daily life. Meeting the Lord at his table is a special time, but he, the living bread, will also meet us when my elderly friend and I sit down to eat our new potatoes and peas.

Prayer: *Dear Lord, while our earnest desire is to honour you in the house of prayer, let us not forget that life itself is an act of worship that gives glory to your name. Amen*

Thought for the day: Christ is the honoured guest in every part of our lives.

Colin D. Harbach (Cumbria, England)

PRAYER FOCUS: TO WELCOME THE LORD AT EVERY MEAL

THURSDAY 16 OCTOBER

More than Enough

Read Exodus 35:20–29

The people were restrained from bringing more, because what they already had was more than enough.
Exodus 36:6–7 (NIV)

Our beloved boss suffered a serious heart attack last winter. As he began recovering at home, I sent out an inter-office request for meals to help his family of eight through this trying time. Generous people signed up, each with a favourite dish—lasagne, beef casserole, curried chicken. After a few weeks, my boss telephoned with the plea, 'Please tell everyone to stop bringing meals. Our refrigerator is overflowing. We have more than enough for days to come!'

Just as my boss had to hold back the generous givers, so did Moses. To help construct the tabernacle, the people willingly donated supplies: a colourful variety of yarns, animal skins, wood, gold jewellery and linen. As they contributed toward the project, they supplied 'more than enough to do all the work' (Exodus 36:7).

My boss was grateful for the outpouring of meals for his family. And I'm sure Moses appreciated the eager givers who helped with the tabernacle. God was surely pleased as well, because 'God loves a cheerful giver' (2 Corinthians 9:7). Working together with willing hearts and faith in God's power, we too can meet seemingly overwhelming needs.

Prayer: *Open our hearts to give joyfully, O God. Move us to become generous to others, just as you are to us. Amen*

Thought for the day: Where can I join with others to provide 'more than enough' for someone in need?

Marion Speicher Brown (Florida, US)

PRAYER FOCUS: ORGANISATIONS BUILDING AFFORDABLE FAMILY HOMES

FRIDAY 17 OCTOBER

The Everlasting Arms

Read Deuteronomy 33:26–29

The eternal God is your refuge, and underneath are the everlasting arms.
Deuteronomy 33:27 (NIV)

This summer I stepped out of my comfort zone and enrolled in an acting class. We began by reading our parts from scripts; the script gave me confidence, and I liked holding it in my hand as I acted my part. But as the class progressed, the class leader asked us to memorise our parts. As I prepared for the opening night, I was terrified I would forget some of my lines.

The day of the performance arrived, and our leader introduced us by saying, 'Tonight, our players are performing without a safety net, so send your positive thoughts out to them.' My heart pounded as I walked onto the stage with no script, feeling exposed and vulnerable.

As I reflected later on our introduction, I realised that in life we never have to perform without a safety net. When Moses led the children of Israel to the brink of the promised land, his final words to them reminded them that through the journey God had been their refuge and strength in unknown territory. No matter what part we are given to play in life and how unfamiliar the stage, God's arms are underneath to uphold, comfort and catch us if we fall.

Prayer: *Dear God, with your everlasting arms underneath, give us courage to step out wherever you call. Amen*

Thought for the day: We are never without the safety net of God's everlasting arms.

Zoe M. Hicks (Georgia, US)

SATURDAY 18 OCTOBER

On the Inside

Read John 10:7–11

[Jesus said] 'I am the door.'
John 10:9 (KJV)

Once, when I was a small boy, we visited my grandparents' house, and I went into the garden to see my grandfather. He welcomed me and chatted to me for a while, and after a pause he reached down and picked up a book, a Bible. He turned over to the place where Jesus speaks of himself as the shepherd, holding out the Bible so I could read it. In the margin I saw the word 'Bruce' and the date. Grandfather said that the last time he had seen Bruce he had read this passage to him and said 'There is one door, but two sides, the inside and the outside. On which side are you?' Bruce had replied, 'I'm on the inside.' Bruce was my cousin, and he had recently been killed in a car accident. I knew that I could not have answered as Bruce had done, though I did not forget what my grandfather had said.

A few years later, I was sitting with my mother in front of the fire on a cold winter's night. When she told me it was time for bed, I got up to give her a goodnight kiss, and she gently held on to my hand. 'Kenneth, would you not like to give your heart to Jesus?' she asked simply. It was the question I had been waiting to be asked, so I replied 'Yes', and there at my mother's knee I did just that. Now, over 80 years later, I can still say with assurance, 'I'm on the inside.'

Prayer: *Dear Lord Jesus, help us to remember that you are the good shepherd who cares for your sheep. Amen*

Thought for the day: Are you on the inside or the outside?

John K. McColl (Stirlingshire, Scotland)

PRAYER FOCUS: PARENTS SPEAKING TO THEIR CHILDREN ABOUT JESUS

SUNDAY 19 OCTOBER

Our Source of Strength

Read Matthew 11:28–30

Carry each other's burdens.
Galatians 6:2 (NIV)

I used to be ashamed of my chronic illness. I pretended that everything was fine, even on days when I couldn't move and it was obvious that something was terribly wrong. I was afraid to admit my need for help or to disclose that I had a disabling condition.

One day, my frustration with having to come up with yet another excuse overwhelmed me, and I started talking to others about my illness. Even though I felt liberated, I feared that I would be shunned or criticised. Instead, something wonderful happened; sharing my brokenness, neediness and weakness caused those around me to open up about the challenging areas in their own lives. When I shared my trials with them, they responded compassionately, helping me to see evidence of God's mercy, power, love and grace in my life.

I realised that being honest about my hardships was a way of encouraging others in their own hardships. And as they told me how God had helped them through tough times, my faith and hope grew stronger. No matter what we are going through, letting others know how God is helping us and strengthening us will bless their lives in ways we can't begin to imagine.

Prayer: *Dear heavenly Father, help us to view our difficult situations as openings through which your glory can shine. Amen*

Thought for the day: Sharing our brokenness can strengthen our faith.

Dorothea M. Love (California, US)

PRAYER FOCUS: THOSE SUFFERING FROM CHRONIC ILLNESS

MONDAY 20 OCTOBER

Using Our Talents

Read 1 Peter 4:7–11
Like good stewards of the manifold grace of God, serve one another with whatever gift each of you has received.
1 Peter 4:10 (NRSV)

My friend told me about an incident from her youth. One day someone brought her a piece of beautiful material from abroad, at a time when a shortage in our country made it impossible to find such cloth for sale. My friend immediately sewed herself a fashionable dress, but she was reluctant to wear it because she felt that she would stand out too much in it. Time passed. She moved the dress from shelf to shelf but never wore it. Hidden from people's eyes for many years, it never served its owner.

This story reminded me of the biblical parable about the talents. One man's talent was not put to good use and brought no benefit to its owner (see Matthew 25:14–30). The same is true of our talents, gifts and potential. If we save up our talents and put them away for future possibilities, they are useless, however precious and valuable they may be. Instead, when we use our talents, God multiplies their benefit—to us and to those we seek to serve.

Prayer: *Dear Lord, you have generously blessed each of us with a special gift or talent. Help us to put our talents to use in serving you and the world. Amen*

Thought for the day: God gave us our talents so we could serve our neighbours.

Irina Ivanova (Pskov, Russia)

PRAYER FOCUS: THOSE SEEKING WAYS TO SERVE

TUESDAY 21 OCTOBER

All about Perspective

Read James 1:2–5

I'm not saying this because I need anything, for I have learned how to be content in any circumstance.
Philippians 4:11 (CEB)

I fly cross-country a lot. Sometimes I admire the majesty of snow-capped mountains, the vast expanse of lush farmland and gorgeous sunrises and sunsets. At other times I focus on the fact that I am squashed in the middle seat between two large men and am embarrassed by nearly falling asleep on a stranger. What is the difference between these two situations? Nothing, really. It's the same plane and the same view. The difference lies in my perspective.

Flying reminds me that we have to let God shape our perspective during the difficult times of life. James teaches us that through our trials we can develop a deeper relationship with God. But if we focus merely on trying to escape the pain of our trials, we might miss God's blessings.

When I fly, I can choose to focus on the beautiful views or on my cramped seating arrangement. Similarly, the way we handle trials determines how much we experience God's triumphant grace in our lives. God told Paul, 'My grace is sufficient for you: for my power is made perfect in weakness.' And Paul chose to 'boast all the more gladly about my weaknesses, so that Christ's power may rest on me' (2 Corinthians 12:9, NIV). When we choose to focus on God's grace, we can draw nearer to him.

Prayer: *Gracious God, help us to view our trials as times when you are trying to teach us more about yourself. Amen*

Thought for the day: The trials we endure can bring us closer to God.

Samuel Winchester (South Carolina, US)

PRAYER FOCUS: FREQUENT FLYERS

WEDNESDAY 22 OCTOBER

Becoming New

Read 2 Corinthians 5:11–21

If anyone is in Christ, that person is part of the new creation. The old things have gone away, and look, new things have arrived!
2 Corinthians 5:17 (CEB)

When I became a Christian at the age of 19, I thought I had to change my personality. I assumed a Christian should be quiet and reserved. For someone like me who was outgoing and loud it was a struggle. I felt that I was supposed to be someone else. But when I grew in age and in faith, I realised that the change I needed was actually a new outlook, focus and vision of the life God had planned for me.

I discovered that God loves us both before and after we become Christians. His children come from all over the world: we look different; we speak different languages; we have different personalities. And that is part of God's big, beautiful plan. When we decide to follow Christ, we know the new change within our hearts is one that comes with great blessing and the true meaning of life.

God made me with this outgoing personality, and that enables me to engage easily with people and invite them to church or Bible study. God made each of us, and we can embrace who we are and confidently be ourselves in his name.

Prayer: *O God, we embrace our newfound life with comfort and joy. Amen*

Thought for the day: God loves us before and after we become Christians.

Cindy Garrard (Florida, US)

PRAYER FOCUS: NEW CHRISTIANS

THURSDAY 23 OCTOBER

Belonging

Read Lamentations 3:22–33

The steadfast love of the Lord never ceases, his mercies never come to an end; they are new every morning; great is your faithfulness.
Lamentations 3:22–23 (NRSV)

Last year my husband and I sold or gave away half of our possessions and moved from the area where we had lived all our lives to a retirement centre hundreds of miles away. Even though we knew the Holy Spirit was present through the whole process, the move was still a traumatic and exhausting ordeal. We had become like strangers in a foreign land.

Last Sunday, however, God's faithfulness enveloped me in joy —I realised we were no longer displaced! Through the year our apprehension of new surroundings has been eclipsed by a sense of belonging among loving neighbours and a vibrant church eager to have new hands and feet to help serve in the name of Jesus Christ. The endless sea of unfamiliar faces is now generously dotted with identifiable smiles of recognition. Concerns about old age and diminished health are met with encouragement and new coping skills.

Today, filled with thanksgiving and courage and God's help, we are considering passing on what we have been given. We intend to answer yes to the call to invite two college-aged foreign exchange students into our lives to help them make the journey from being strangers to belonging. Each day we anticipate a new sign of God's faithfulness.

Prayer: *Dear Lord, thank you for your mercies, blessings and faithfulness. In Jesus' name we pray. Amen*

Thought for the day: Each day brings new signs of God's faithfulness.

Cindy Love (Texas, US)

PRAYER FOCUS: NEW RETIREES

FRIDAY 24 OCTOBER

Water for the Thirsty

Read John 4:1–26
The king will say to those on his right, '… I was thirsty and you gave me something to drink.'
Matthew 25:34–35 (NIV)

One hot, humid summer afternoon I was sitting on my patio when I heard a delivery truck approaching our cul-de-sac. I watched as the driver knocked on my neighbour's door. Mary greeted him with a smile, took a small parcel and then said to him, 'Would you like a glass of cold water?' The driver eagerly accepted her kind offer.

As this scene of Christian love and service unfolded before my eyes, I recalled how Jesus had declared that his kingdom people would be marked by their deeds of mercy, like giving a drink to a thirsty person. A simple gesture like that, he explained, was like giving a drink to him. After the driver pulled away, I went next door and thanked Mary for what she had done. She told me, 'After the driver thanked me he said, "God bless you", and I told him I believe in Jesus, and he said he did, too.'

Their conversation caused me to ask myself, 'How many opportunities like this come my way, and I fail to do something as simple as offering water to a thirsty worker?' Mary's example reminds me that Christ's followers need always to be ready to offer both the water that quenches our thirst and the water of eternal life that Jesus gives to a thirsty world.

Prayer: *Dear God, remind us to supply those in need with sustenance for their bodies but also the water of life that brings salvation to all who believe. Amen*

Thought for the day: We serve Jesus by showing deeds of kindness and mercy to others.

Jim Reapsome (Illinois, US)

PRAYER FOCUS: DELIVERY WORKERS

SATURDAY 25 OCTOBER

Mornings with God

Read Psalm 1:1–3

Their delight is in the law of the Lord, and on his law they meditate day and night.
Psalm 1:2 (NRSV)

I woke up and immediately started rehearsing my to-do list for the day. Sprinkled throughout my mental list were worries and concerns about my family. The things to do and family cares seemed to assault my whole body, not just my mind. My neck muscles tensed up, and my mind could not focus even on my waking-up routine.

I reached for the Bible and sat up in my bed. Focusing on reading the Bible and *The Upper Room* daily meditation began to dissolve the stress I felt. I continued to read and then to write in my journal. I finished with prayer.

After spending this time with God, I still had my to-do list, but I had more perspective on it. Tomorrow might yield another to-do list; but if I handle it with God, through prayer and meditation, it will be manageable.

Prayer: *Ever-present God, when the cares of our lives press in on us, quieten our minds enough to focus on you. Amen*

Thought for the day: Reaching for God's word in the morning helps us face the day.

Norma P. Marroquin (Texas, US)

PRAYER FOCUS: THOSE OVERWHELMED BY DAILY CONCERNS

SUNDAY 26 OCTOBER

'People Like Him'

Read Matthew 7:1–5

There is no one on earth who is righteous, no one who does what is right and never sins.
Ecclesiastes 7:20 (NIV)

For years I worked for a prison ministry, training Christians to share God's love with inmates. I also spoke to secular groups about problems that prisoners face.

During those years, a man was arrested in my home town and convicted of grisly crimes, including the murders of 15 young men. For months the sensational story with its shocking details made headlines. People often approached me after my presentations, mentioned this man, and said, 'You don't have anything to do with people like him, do you?' Their tone implied that, while sharing God's love with some prisoners might be acceptable, there was a degree of evil beyond which even God should not intervene. I was saddened that it was not only at secular gatherings that I encountered this attitude; sometimes I heard it in churches too.

Too often we are quick to rank sins, forgetting that everyone sins and that all sin is abhorrent to God. We seem unable—or, worse, unwilling—to believe that the blood of Christ can cleanse *any* repentant person from *any* sin. As forgiven people, we should be eager to share God's grace with everyone.

Prayer: *Dear Lord, help us to forgive, even as you have forgiven us. Amen*

Thought for the day: Christ can forgive any sin.

Lisa Stackpole (Wisconsin, US)

PRAYER FOCUS: PRISON MINISTRIES

MONDAY 27 OCTOBER

God the Craftsman

Read Exodus 35:30–35

We are God's handiwork, created in Christ Jesus to do good works.
Ephesians 2:10 (NIV)

I watched the craftsman as he made a beautiful piece of furniture in his workshop. He took his time, carefully making each cut and standing back now and then to look at his work. Some companies mass-produce their work and make money, but the master craftsman concerns himself with creating a thing of beauty and integrity. He may never be rich, but he has great satisfaction.

God chose Bezalel and Oholiab to make artistic designs for the tabernacle. He filled them with skill, ability and knowledge. God himself is a craftsman whose divine spirit gave these men the ability to make beautiful things. The beautiful furnishings of the tabernacle were unseen by most people, but God saw and was pleased.

The apostle Paul says that we believers are God's workmanship, created in Christ Jesus to do good works. And God never does a shoddy job. The hand of the Craftsman is at work in us and through us shaping us to be more like Christ.

Prayer: *Because it is you, dear God, at work in us, we know we can do the works you have prepared for us to do. We pray as Jesus taught us, saying, 'Our Father which art in heaven, Hallowed be thy name. Thy kingdom come. Thy will be done, as in heaven, so in earth. Give us day by day our daily bread. And forgive us our sins; for we also forgive every one that is indebted to us. And lead us not into temptation; but deliver us from evil.'* Amen*

Thought for the day: Even when we can't see it, God is working in our lives.

Marion Turnbull (Liverpool, England)

PRAYER FOCUS: FURNITURE MAKERS
* Luke 11:2–4 (KJV)

TUESDAY 28 OCTOBER

Camp Grace

Read John 15:8–17

The Spirit helps us in our weakness; for we do not know how to pray as we ought, but that very Spirit intercedes with sighs too deep for words.
Romans 8:26 (NRSV)

For three decades, adults with special needs, along with many volunteers, have attended Camp Grace in the mountains of North Carolina. At this 'family reunion' I have found the campers' love for one another and their love and acceptance of me very moving. The highlight is Saturday's talent show in which nearly all the campers select a talent to share.

Susan, who rarely speaks, usually dances. However, this year, she wanted to sing 'Jesus loves me'. She stood, quite anxious, in front of the microphone, and said, 'Hi.' As our accompanist quietly tried to prompt her with the words, she said 'Hi' again. At that, voices began to arise from Susan's Camp Grace family, until we were all singing 'Jesus loves me' softly and sweetly, on her behalf. Susan grinned as she received our love and affirmation and knew she was not alone.

Through the Holy Spirit, God was illustrating Romans 8:26. When Christ ascended, he left us a Comforter who intervenes for us with God when we struggle. As we lifted Susan's song to God, we were bearing the fruit of God's love (see John 15:16–17).

Prayer: *Dear Lord, help us to bring your comfort to others in their times of hardship. Amen*

Thought for the day: Jesus loves me.

Daniel R. Nelson (North Carolina, US)

PRAYER FOCUS: PEOPLE WITH SPECIAL NEEDS

WEDNESDAY 29 OCTOBER

Keep Your Hands Up

Read Exodus 17:8–13
Aaron and Hur held up [Moses'] hands, one on one side, and the other on the other side.
Exodus 17:12 (NRSV)

During rehabilitation for drug addiction, I accepted Christ as my Saviour and invited him into my life. When I had completed rehab I found it difficult to find work. I did not have much money, and a sea of temptations—both new and old—surrounded me. Then my mother fell seriously ill. At times I was in despair and on the verge of a breakdown. I prayed, but it seemed as if I was receiving no answer or support from God. However, that was not the case.

God directed me to a church where the brothers and sisters welcomed me joyfully. They prayed for me, empathised with me, helped me in whatever ways they could and strengthened me with their words and faith and encouragement. The pastor said, 'Keep your hands up (a Russian expression meaning 'Don't give up'). All will be well. You can do it. God will support you and we—your family—will be close at hand.' The youth group helped to decorate the flat where I lived with my mother, and when she died the whole church supported me.

Now I am serving as a deacon in the church and try to be near those who need my help—so I can hold up their hands.

Prayer: *Dear God of encouragement, help us to see those people who need our support, and then to give it to them wholeheartedly. Amen*

Thought for the day: God acts through us in this world.

Stanislav Prokhorov (Samara, Russia)

PRAYER FOCUS: THOSE STRUGGLING WITH ADDICTIONS

THURSDAY 30 OCTOBER

Pull Out That Weed!

Read Romans 12:14–21

See to it that no one fails to obtain the grace of God; that no root of bitterness springs up and causes trouble, and through it many become defiled.

Hebrews 12:15 (NRSV)

After examining the roses I had planted again this year, I was not disappointed. In all their varied colours they had burst into bloom. These lovely flowers had never failed to spread out quickly to fill my flowerbed.

Then I took a closer look to see that some of the space was filled with a weed that looked a lot like a rose, but is a real troublemaker and difficult to pull out. After I had thoroughly weeded the flowerbed, I had to watch for those nasty weeds springing up again. They hadn't finished making trouble for me!

The Bible tells us about a weed that, if allowed to grow and develop in our lives, will cause us lots of trouble. If bitterness takes hold, we will use words that hurt others instead of helping and healing them. The only way to get rid of bitterness is to pull it out by the root. And to do that, we need God's help. When we ask him to clean bitterness from our lives, we must watch and pray, or it might spring up again. Removing bitterness allows love and forgiveness to spread and makes life beautiful again.

Prayer: *O God, take our bitterness and replace it with love and kindness. May your love spread to those around us. Amen*

Thought for the day: Tending the garden of life with prayer will produce the blooms of a beautiful spirit.

Shirley Myers (New York, US)

PRAYER FOCUS: GARDENERS

FRIDAY 31 OCTOBER

'Don't Give Up'

Read Isaiah 38:1–5

Lord… You restored me to health and let me live.
Isaiah 38:16 (NIV)

King Hezekiah was 'at the point of death' because of his illness. But he recovered with God's help. Hezekiah's story reminds me of an illness from which God helped me to recover.

Mine was a mental illness. Several years ago loneliness, financial struggles and work problems felt like relentless adversaries, and I began having suicidal thoughts. I wanted relief from my emotional pain and came to believe that suicide would be the way to attain it.

As I headed toward the garage where I parked my car one night, I was thinking about the note I had scribbled on yellow-lined paper and various methods of carbon monoxide poisoning. When I reached my car, I noticed a laminated prayer card on the pavement beside the driver's door. It was titled, 'Don't Give Up'.

I could taste my salty tears as I read it. Despite the fact that I had not involved God in any aspect of my life, I felt him reaching out to me through that prayer card. The following morning, I contacted a doctor. With counselling and medication I recovered from my illness, and a few months later a pastor led me to Jesus. I keep that prayer card in my kitchen as a reminder that God values our lives and 'saves those who are crushed in spirit' (Psalm 34:18, NIV).

Prayer: *Heavenly Father, we praise you for your divine mercy when illness steals our health and hope. Amen*

Thought for the day: Don't give up.

Debra Pierce (Massachusetts, US)

PRAYER FOCUS: PEOPLE SUFFERING FROM MENTAL ILLNESS

Prayer Workshop

Listening

Jesus spent the whole night in communion. The way I would like to define communion here is that Jesus spent the night listening to the Father calling him the Beloved. That is the voice Jesus heard when he came up out of the Jordan River 'You are my Son, the Beloved; with you I am well pleased' (Luke 3:22, NRSV), and he hears that same voice on the mountain: 'This is my Son, my Chosen, listen to him!' (Luke 9:35). It is with this knowledge of being the Beloved that Jesus could walk freely into a world in which he was not treated as the Beloved. People applauded him, laughed at him, praised him and rejected him. They called out 'Hosanna!' and they called out 'Crucify!' But in the midst of all those voices, Jesus knew one thing—'I am the Beloved; I am God's favourite one.'

Why is it so important that we are with God and God alone on the mountaintop? It's important because it's the place in which we can listen to the voice of the One who calls us the beloved. Jesus says to you and to me that we are loved as he is loved. That same voice is there for us. To pray is to let that voice speak to the centre of our being and permeate our whole life. 'Who am I?' I am the beloved. If we are not claiming that voice as the deepest truth of our being, then we cannot walk freely in this world...

This listening is not easy. Jesus spent the *night* in prayer. God's voice is not a voice we always hear with physical ears. God's word is not always an insight that suddenly comes to us in our minds or that satisfies our hearts...

That is where the discipline of prayer comes in. We are called to pray not because we feel like praying or because it gives us great insights, but simply because we want to be obedient, to listen to the voice that calls us the beloved. The word 'listen' in Latin is *audire*. If we listen with full attention in which we are totally geared to listen, it's called *obaudire*, and that's where the word 'obedience' comes from. Jesus is the obedient one—totally open to the love of God.

And if we are closed, and to the degree that we are closed, we are *surdus*. That is the Latin word for 'deaf'. The more 'deaf' we get, the more *absurdus* we become, and an absurd life is precisely a life in which we no longer listen and are constantly distracted by all sorts of voices and lose touch with the truth that we are the beloved…

Real freedom to live in this world comes from hearing clearly the truth about who we are, which is that we are the beloved. That's what prayer is about. And that's why it is so crucial and not just a nice thing to do once in a while. It is the essential attitude that creates in us the freedom to love other people not because they are going to love us back but because we are so loved, and out of the abundance of that love we want to give.

This is where ministry starts, because our freedom is anchored in claiming our belovedness. Being the beloved allows us to go into this world and touch people, heal them, speak with them and make them aware that they too are beloved, chosen and blessed. It is an incredible mystery of God's love that the more we know how deeply we are loved, the more we will see how deeply our sisters and our brothers in the human family are loved.

But we have to pray. We have to listen to the voice that calls us the beloved.

Questions for Reflection:

1. When was the last time you spent time alone, listening for God? What was that experience like?

2. When have you most clearly felt beloved by God? Who or what helped you to recognise God's love for you?

3. Knowing you are God's beloved child, whom will you reach out to today? Who most needs to hear of God's love from you?

This prayer workshop was adapted from *A Spirituality of Living*, part of the Henri J. M. Nouwen Spirituality series published by Upper Room Books. Henri Nouwen was an internationally renowned author, respected professor and beloved pastor. He wrote over 40 books on the spiritual life and, since his death in 1996, people seeking a deeper relationship with God have turned to his writings for direction.

SATURDAY 1 NOVEMBER

Whose Am I?

Read Galatians 5:22–25

Jesus said, 'If you really know me, you will know my Father as well.'
John 14:7 (NIV)

One of our neighbours recently spent three months hammering away making a playhouse. His four-year-old son joined him in this building project and the two worked with gusto. Like father, like son!

As I think of the way this son imitates his father, I wonder if my actions, habits and preferences reflect my heavenly Father. I ask myself if people who know me can recognise something of the Father in me. Do my words and actions show the influence of the Holy Spirit in my life? Does my life reflect the teachings of Jesus? Am I faithful, patient and loving—not just on a good day, but every day?

If my Christianity is 'real', I will reflect my Father to the people around me. That's a big challenge—and responsibility—for each of us.

Prayer: *Loving Father, we want to be like you. We want to help others get to know you better. Help us to work toward reflecting you in all our words and actions. Amen*

Thought for the day: Jesus reflected the Father to those around him, and so can I.

Meg Mangan (New South Wales, Australia)

PRAYER FOCUS: FATHERS AND SONS

SUNDAY 2 NOVEMBER

Communion of Saints

Read 2 Timothy 1:1–14

Since we are surrounded by so great a cloud of witnesses, let us also lay aside every weight and the sin that clings so closely, and let us run with perseverance the race that is set before us.
Hebrews 12:1 (NRSV)

I love All Saints Day, when we celebrate the saints among us who have gone on to heavenly glory. During worship that day we read the names of those who have died in the faith since the previous year. As their pastor, I have powerful memories of the many people whose names are read, memories of stories and experiences and prayers we shared—holy moments. These people are examples of lives well lived, and so it is right for me to honour the memory of those—such as my parents and my grandparents—who have contributed so richly to who I am.

Maybe I love this Sunday so much because it is the Christian Church's way of announcing to the world that there is a glorious heaven and that Jesus is the one true light to lead us there. We who believe know absolutely, for certain, things that non-believers cannot know. Maybe I love it because of the time of Holy Communion when I am aware of that phrase we say in the Apostles' Creed: 'I believe in the communion of saints'. Each time I strongly feel surrounded by the 'great a cloud of witnesses'. That's why I love this Sunday.

Prayer: *Dear God, help us live in gratitude for all the faithful ones who have gone before us. May we follow their example in living so that others come to know Christ. Amen*

Thought for the day: Every day, each one of us stands in company with all the saints.

Dan Johnson (Florida, US)

PRAYER FOCUS: THOSE WHO MODEL THE FAITH FOR ME

MONDAY 3 NOVEMBER

Infinite Compassion

Read Matthew 11:28–30

Are not five sparrows sold for two pennies? Yet not one of them is forgotten in God's sight.
Luke 12:6 (NRSV)

My elderly husband's eyesight was deteriorating and my own responsibilities as his carer were increasing. I began to feel completely overlooked. I understood that my husband was at the forefront of everyone's concerns, but on one particular day I felt I was regarded only as an attachment to him rather than a person in my own right.

In my daily Bible reading and prayers that night, I didn't ask for any help from God. However, as I was falling asleep, the thought came to me: Jesus values me as no one else does. He knows me personally and loves me. I had been taught this for most of my life, yet only at this moment did the thought really hit home. It was so comforting and empowering and came at a time when I most needed strength to cope with the challenges ahead.

Looking back, I marvel at God's generosity in restoring my feelings of confidence and self-worth. God knew my needs and helped me before I even asked.

Because God is boundlessly compassionate to us we can show compassion to those around us. We can rely on God's spirit to guide and direct us in what we say and do.

Prayer: *Dear Lord, help us to feel your compassion for us each day. Make us sensitive to the needs of others, whether spoken or unspoken. Amen*

Thought for the day: All the kindness we give or receive shows God's compassion.

Margaret Elizabeth Gregory (Hertfordshire, England)

PRAYER FOCUS: CARERS

TUESDAY 4 NOVEMBER

Finished with Shame and Guilt

Read John 19:28–30

If anyone is in Christ, there is a new creation: everything old has passed away; see, everything has become new!
2 Corinthians 5:17 (NRSV)

My mother worked, assembling heaters, to support her four children. At the weekends, Mama consoled herself by drinking until she was drunk. On weeknights, she released her frustrations by wielding a leather belt as punishment when her children left a chore undone, argued with each other or questioned an order. Mama's angst led to poor choices: an abusive boyfriend, isolation from her parents and other family, and drug and alcohol abuse, which eventually contributed to her death.

I continued the pattern of making poor choices, which mired me in shame and guilt. I chose alcohol and drugs over spiritual and personal development, isolation over community, taking instead of giving. I longed to be set free. One day, sitting in a cold, grey cement-block cell, I found freedom as I read about Jesus' dying on the cross. I realised that Jesus made a choice to save me from my bad choices. The Saviour's final words, 'It is finished' (John 19:30), mean that I am saved from sin and from sin's damaging by-products: shame, guilt and anxiety.

When we truly believe this, we can be set free from the hurts, hang-ups and bad habits that keep us from becoming the people God intended us to be.

Prayer: *Dear God, help us to understand that Jesus' death and resurrection mean that we are set free from bondage. Amen*

Thought for the day: In Christ we are free from shame and guilt.

Avon White (Tennessee, US)

PRAYER FOCUS: THOSE WHO FEEL DEFEATED BY PAST MISTAKES

WEDNESDAY 5 NOVEMBER

Taking the Lead

Read Psalm 139:5–10
If a blind person leads another blind person, both will fall into a ditch.
Matthew 15:14 (CEB)

When my friends and I tried ballroom dancing, we knew the roles: the men lead and the women follow. Growing up as an American woman, I believe women should never subject themselves to man's dominance. However, as I came to enjoy the complementary dance roles of leader and follower and considered how God desires to lead us, I realised that I may have mistaken leading as dominance, to my detriment.

In ballroom dancing, the man's purpose is to empower his partner to express beauty, elegance and grace. He surveys their surroundings, determines their course and guides the woman by gently pressing his hand against her back. I'll never forget one partner who failed to keep his hand strong and purposeful. I was constantly looking over my shoulder in fear we might crash. However, with a partner who confidently took the lead—careful to guide and protect my steps—I felt safe and was free to enjoy the dance.

Likewise, God desires to lead us, not to dominate us. Because we are made in his image, when we yield ourselves to his loving lead, we reflect his beauty and grace back to a fearful, lost and chaotic world.

Prayer: *Dear Lord, teach us to follow your lead that we may guide others into the truth of your love. Amen*

Thought for the day: God's leading is strong and sure.

Shadia Hrichi (California, US)

PRAYER FOCUS: DANCERS

THURSDAY 6 NOVEMBER

Love God; Love People

Read John 14:15–31

'Love the Lord your God with all your heart and with all your soul and with all your mind and with all your strength' [and...] 'Love your neighbour as yourself.' There is no commandment greater than these.
Mark 12:30–31 (NIV)

Worship at the campsite brought those who attended closer together in the name of Jesus. Our surroundings were simple. We had no fancy pews, sound equipment or lighting. Many denominations were represented. We gathered together because we loved God and were thankful for Jesus Christ.

Being a Christian is easier than we often make it. We are called to love the Lord our God and to love our neighbours as ourselves. When we love God, we want to know him better and to develop a stronger, more personal relationship with the Lord. The more we work on our relationship with God, the more the Holy Spirit works in us to make us the people God wants us to be. The more we allow the Holy Spirit to work in us, the more we love other people. If all Christians strive to love God and people, think of the amazing things we can do to further God's kingdom and proclaim the gospel of Jesus Christ.

Prayer: *Dear God, when our lives get complicated, remind us to focus on the simplicity of your message to love you and our neighbours; in Jesus' name. Amen*

Thought for the day: Love God; love people.

Bev Hurlburt (Ohio, US)

FRIDAY 7 NOVEMBER

'Pray for Me'

Read James 5:13–20

The prayer of the righteous is powerful and effective.
James 5:16 (NRSV)

Last year was a period of trials and tribulations for my family and me. Even though I maintain a healthy lifestyle, I began to feel unwell. My wife and daughter urged me to visit the doctor, who quickly diagnosed several problems: high levels of sugar, urea and creatinine in my blood, and an enlarged heart. He informed me that these conditions could cause blindness, stroke and heart attack at any time.

Treatment began immediately with medication and a very strict diet. But more importantly, I asked people to pray for me. My family, our friends, church members and people from far away prayed for me. Indeed, my healing has become a powerful example of faith, even to friends of other faiths, including my doctor. Some even wrote letters to say, 'Your faith has helped to increase our faith.' Praise the Lord!

A praying Christian community is a worshipping community. When we pray together, we bring love, faith, hope, peace and justice to the world.

Prayer: *Dear God, increase our faith and help us to proclaim that Jesus is the way, the truth and the life we seek. Amen*

Thought for the day: Praying for one another is a powerful testimony of our faith.

Komal Masih (Uttar Pradesh, India)

PRAYER FOCUS: PEOPLE WHO PRAY FOR ME

SATURDAY 8 NOVEMBER

When Plans Change

Read Luke 10:25–37

The human mind plans the way, but the Lord directs the steps.
Proverbs 16:9 (NRSV)

Peggy was home on holiday, and I looked forward to having coffee with her. When she didn't arrive on time, I wondered what was keeping her. I knew she didn't have a mobile phone and couldn't contact me. Eventually, I began to lose patience. Finally she arrived, appearing unhurried, and she apologised for the delay. She explained she had been talking with someone who had revealed a deep need. Peggy took 'our' time to respond, trusting that I would understand.

Admiration replaced my annoyance. Like the good Samaritan, Peggy did what she could to bring comfort to someone in need. I asked her, 'But how did you deal with your own feelings about being late?'

Peggy replied, 'I've learned to trust God with it.'

Now when, through no fault of my own, I'm running late and have notified others of my dilemma, I'm learning to believe God is at work wherever I am going. Often, I learn the people affected were either delayed themselves, or something came up to make the change welcome. Delays are inevitable, but we have a choice; we can either act with frustration or believe that God is directing our steps. Choosing to trust his timing produces peace.

Prayer: *Dear Lord, we put today in your hands. Help us to believe that you will order our lives as we trust you with them. Amen*

Thought for the day: Today's plans are subject to change at God's direction.

Ellen M. Cardwell (California, US)

PRAYER FOCUS: TO BE OPEN TO INTERRUPTIONS

SUNDAY 9 NOVEMBER

God Heals

Read 1 Chronicles 16:28–36
Give thanks to the Lord, for he is good; his love endures forever.
1 Chronicles 16:34 (NIV)

Years ago I was called to return to hospital to receive a second kidney transplant. I had been on kidney dialysis for two long stretches of time and had received my brother's kidney a year earlier. I had his kidney for a short time, and then my body rejected it and it had to be removed. I lost part of my hearing from the rejection process. Then I went back on dialysis.

A few weeks later I received a second kidney. It was a kidney from a man who was killed in a midwestern city. He had a card in his wallet saying that his body could be used for medical purposes if he died.

I have had that transplanted kidney for almost 35 years, and I have been healthy the entire time. I am thankful for the transplant and for the donor who gave me many more years of a happy life because of his willingness to carry a donor card in his wallet. I believe that God has healed me and every day I give thanks. Now I go to the dialysis units in my city to offer hope and encouragement to those having treatment.

Prayer: *Dear God, thank you for calling us to serve you every day in the name of Jesus Christ. Amen*

Thought for the day: Today I will thank God for my life.

Lyndon C. Weberg (Arizona, US)

PRAYER FOCUS: THOSE AWAITING ORGAN TRANSPLANTS

MONDAY 10 NOVEMBER

Feeling Alone?

Read Romans 12:9–16
Be of the same mind one toward another.
Romans 12:16 (KJV)

My mum died when I was almost four, so my dad and great-grandmother raised my siblings and me. Because of my loss, I always felt like an outcast at school. But my outlook on life changed dramatically towards the end of my schooldays. Until then, I had never met another student who had lost his or her mother. I will always remember my response when I heard one of my classmates reading out an essay. As part of it, she mentioned that her mum had died. I tried to listen carefully and absorb what she was saying. I remember how glad I was to know someone who had experienced the same type of loss that I had. That single encounter changed the way I viewed my mother's death.

I believe sometimes in our spiritual lives we want to find someone who feels the same way we do about God. Whether at home, school or work, we want to be understood. Fellowship is a powerful tool that can be used to foster communication with others and to serve God. I am grateful that God loves us enough to allow others to cross our path at just the right time.

Prayer: *Dear Lord, thank you for allowing us to share our lives with others. May our story lead others to you. Amen*

Thought for the day: God can use me today to help someone feeling alone or in need.

Tara Regina Lyle (Mississippi, US)

TUESDAY 11 NOVEMBER

Soul Rest

Read Psalm 62:1–8

Truly my soul finds rest in God.
Psalm 62:1 (NIV)

When I was in the Marines, I was required to carry heavy equipment or supplies strapped to my back. I remember distinctly the feeling of lightness and relief when I was allowed to lay that burden down. Suddenly, I felt light as a feather.

We carry through this world two types of burdens: physical and spiritual. Physical burdens weigh us down, sap our strength and weary our bodies. Spiritual burdens—worries, fears, sorrows—weigh us down mentally and emotionally. Psalm 62:8 points the way for us to lay down our spiritual burdens and find rest for our souls.

How do we enter into the soul's rest of which the psalmist writes? Through our relationship with God, by trusting in him and pouring out our hearts to him in prayer, we find comfort, peace of mind and freedom from fear and worry. Then we lay our burdens down and go on our way, lightened, refreshed and encouraged.

Remember: God already knows what is in our hearts, so we are not informing the Lord of our cares and burdens when we seek him in prayer. We are laying our burdens upon the Lord so that we no longer need to carry them ourselves.

Prayer: *Dear God, help us to take full advantage of your offer of rest for our souls; and remind us that when we rest in your strength, nothing can shake us. Amen*

Thought for the day: God invites us to lay down our burdens.

DeVonna R. Allison (Michigan, US)

PRAYER FOCUS: MILITARY VETERANS

WEDNESDAY 12 NOVEMBER

The Gift

Read 1 John 5:11–12

Thanks be to God for his indescribable gift!
2 Corinthians 9:15 (NIV)

I opened the present slowly. This gift, one of many I'd received from a close friend over the years, would be as thoughtful and extravagant as the others. She knows me well. She is quite aware of all my failings and strengths, and she loves me in spite of them. For a moment, I hesitated. Knowing I could never give her anything as expensive in return, I considered handing the gift back to her. But as I searched her face, filled with the expectancy of my joy, I couldn't deny her the pleasure. The gift would benefit both of us.

For many years, I have chosen to reject the lavish gift of forgiveness that God gave me through the blood of Jesus. I considered it a debt I must try to repay. The guilt was unbearable, the weight on my self-esteem heavy. But on that day, sitting with my friend, I understood. I'd caught a glimpse of Jesus in her eyes. The gift of his magnificent sacrifice and his offer of eternal life gives him pleasure, despite my unworthiness. The fact that I can never repay him is irrelevant.

'For God so loved the world that he gave his one and only Son, that whoever believes in him shall not perish but have eternal life' (John 3:16). All we need to do is to say, 'Thank you.'

Prayer: *Every day, dear God, you present us with new gifts. Bless us with eyes to see and accept them graciously. Amen*

Thought for the day: We are blessed when we open God's gifts.

Heidi Gaul (Oregon, US)

PRAYER FOCUS: FAITHFUL FRIENDS

THURSDAY 13 NOVEMBER

Desert Experience

Read John 4:1–15

The Lord says, 'I will pour water on the thirsty land and streams on the dry ground; I will pour my spirit on your descendants, and my blessing on your offspring.'

Isaiah 44:3 (NRSV)

My country, Australia, has a large arid centre. Running right through this centre from north to south is a network of rivers, which can be dry for years on end. This year, monsoonal rains in the north shed vast quantities of water into the catchment area for these rivers. Slowly, inexorably, the water began to flow south toward a great dry lakebed, Lake Ayre.

As the channels filled, new life appeared. Trees and shrubs flourished; grass sprang up; flowers bloomed. Animals and birds gathered. In Lake Ayre, myriad waterfowl flocked in to feed and breed. Life abounded again in the desert.

God assured his people that he would pour out on them the water of life and Jesus came offering 'living water' to all who received him. The same is true today. Renewed spiritually, lives blossom in Christ. Whoever believes in him becomes a source of 'living water' (John 7:38) for others. When we allow the Holy Spirit to direct us into acts of mercy, faith and love, we reveal the abundant life (John 10:10) welling up in us.

Prayer: *Dear Lord, help us each day to reveal your life-giving presence to people we meet. Amen*

Thought for the day: Christ's presence can renew anyone.

Everard Blackman (Queensland, Australia)

PRAYER FOCUS: PEOPLE LIVING IN DESERT AREAS

FRIDAY 14 NOVEMBER

A Change of Plans

Read Isaiah 55:10–13

I trusted in thee, O Lord; I said, Thou art my God. My times are in thy hand.
Psalm 31:14–15 (KJV)

While I was preparing for work, the phone rang. The message said that schools in my area were closed again because of the wintry weather. I was thankful that students and teachers would not have to travel on icy roads. But as a teacher I had worked hard to prepare lessons for my students—lessons I would not be able to teach.

In my frustration, I remembered the verse from Psalm 31 which says, 'My times are in thy hand.' I began to think of the day before me in a new way. How could I best use this time? Possibilities formed in my mind, including quiet time for prayer, scripture reading and writing my journal. I also found time for some neglected household chores. Frequently I looked out at the falling snow and admired the beauty of God's world. My frustration turned to contentment as the day became filled with meaningful moments.

Ecclesiastes 9:10 tells us, 'Whatsoever thy hand findeth to do, do it with thy might.' I wasn't teaching, and the day did not go as I had planned. But, through God's guidance, I still spent time doing meaningful work. After all, my times are always in God's hands.

Prayer: *Dear God, help us to remember that when our days don't go as we plan, you are still at work in life's events. Help us to trust you throughout each day of our life. Amen*

Thought for the day: Our times are in God's hands, even when the days don't go as we plan.

Deborah Ross (North Carolina, US)

SATURDAY 15 NOVEMBER

Keeping a Record

Read Philippians 4:4–7

I call on the Lord in my distress, and he answers me.
Psalm 120:1 (NIV)

I can't count the number of times the psalmist's experience with prayer has been true for me. Keeping a record of answered prayers helps me call to mind quickly and easily instances when God unmistakably said yes.

It is important that we keep a record of answered prayer because we need encouragement from day to day. The best encouragement comes when we remember the good things God has done for us. As he has been faithful in the past, so he will be faithful now—and tomorrow. God doesn't change. He is not fickle.

Whatever troubles we are experiencing today, we can take them to God. When we cry out to our Creator, as the psalmist did, he hears our prayers. Then in absolute trust we can believe that he will answer us.

Prayer: *Dear Father, help us to remember and be grateful for everything you have done in our lives. We pray as Jesus taught us, saying, 'Our Father which art in heaven, Hallowed be thy name. Thy kingdom come. Thy will be done, as in heaven, so in earth. Give us day by day our daily bread. And forgive us our sins; for we also forgive every one that is indebted to us. And lead us not into temptation; but deliver us from evil.'* Amen*

Thought for the day: God is faithful and will answer when we call.

David Bowman (Texas, US)

PRAYER FOCUS: GRATITUDE FOR GOD'S FAITHFULNESS
* Luke 11:2–4 (KJV)

SUNDAY 16 NOVEMBER

Closer to God

Read Mark 12:41–44
If I give all I possess to the poor… but do not have love, I gain nothing.
1 Corinthians 13:3 (NIV)

Recently we completed our church stewardship campaign. This consisted of a series of messages, starting with the big picture of living for Christ. We then discussed how stewardship fits into a life that is pleasing to God, including the Bible's guidance on managing money.

As stewardship chair, I set up a meeting with our minister before the campaign began to discuss how we would determine the success of the campaign. I expected his response to be something along the lines of a 5 per cent increase in total giving, or perhaps more people pledging money this year than last. But when I asked the question, I was surprised at his answer. He said his view of success would be seeing people move closer to God. The more I reflected on his response, the more I realised he was right.

The widow in today's story gave generously, and Jesus commended her for it. I honestly believe that God doesn't care how much we give, but *how* we give—from the heart, joyfully, with a desire to move closer to him as an act of trust. If we are moving closer to God—in our worship, prayer, service and witness—then our joyful, generous giving will follow as a natural expression of our thanks to him for all he gives to us.

Prayer: *O God, teach us to give joyfully so that we move ever closer to you. Amen*

Thought for the day: Generous giving expresses our thanks to God.

John D. Bown (Minnesota, US)

PRAYER FOCUS: STEWARDSHIP COMMITTEES

MONDAY 17 NOVEMBER

Muzzling My Mouth

Read Ephesians 4:25–32

Do not let any unwholesome talk come out of your mouths, but only what is helpful for building others up according to their needs, that it may benefit those who listen.

Ephesians 4:29 (NIV)

Years ago, I adopted a dog that had a fear of strangers. Whenever the vet examined her, he muzzled her so she couldn't bite him. At times, I wish someone would put a muzzle on my mouth—such as the time I berated a woman who was talking loudly on her mobile phone. Immediately Psalm 39:1 came to mind: 'I will watch my ways and keep my tongue from sin: I will put a muzzle on my mouth.' If the psalmist had the self-control to keep his mouth shut, why don't I?

Even when I do manage to keep my mouth shut, I seethe in silence. But that is sin waiting to happen. I've learned that living righteously and keeping my mouth from sin requires a lot of close communication with God. 'Lord, put a muzzle over my mouth' has become a frequent prayer of mine. Whenever I'm feeling irritated, I ask God to calm me. I ask him to give me the strength to conduct myself with gentleness. I still make mistakes and allow angry words to roll off my lips. I sometimes speak in a tone that is offensive. But my convicted spirit prompts me to confess my sin to God and ask forgiveness. Then I ask him to strengthen my commitment to speak with kindness and self-control the next time anger or frustration tries to get the better of me.

Prayer: *Dear heavenly Father, may our words be used for goodness, grace and godliness. Amen*

Thought for the day: God's love can transform our words of anger into words for good.

Debra Pierce (Massachusetts, US)

PRAYER FOCUS: THOSE WHO ARE EASILY ANGERED

TUESDAY 18 NOVEMBER

Compassion

Read Mark 1:40–45

Jesus was indignant. He reached out his hand and touched the man. 'I am willing,' he said. 'Be clean!'
Mark 1:41 (NIV)

Many years ago a neighbour lost one of her children through a tragic accident. I didn't know her well, but due to the unusual circumstances of this child's death, I cried for days. Finally, after several weeks had passed, I wrote to my neighbour and was surprised to receive a return note. She said that messages like the one I had sent brought an occasional ray of sunshine to her day. Each year since that exchange, I have sent a note near the anniversary of her child's death and one near his birthday.

Once on a chance meeting she hugged me and said, 'Never let those cards stop coming. Everyone else forgets.' She expressed gratitude that, even years later, someone could still share the grief that she never forgets.

Jesus was a man who understood compassion, and he taught us to share it with others. Sometimes that compassion is as simple as sharing a hug, a note, a listening ear and the love of Jesus.

Prayer: *Compassionate Father, you know our pain. By your grace we can move forward when life hurts. Thank you for your healing touch. Amen*

Thought for the day: Jesus calls us to show compassion.

Margie Harding (Maryland, US)

PRAYER FOCUS: PARENTS GRIEVING FOR A CHILD

WEDNESDAY 19 NOVEMBER

In Prayer

Read Psalm 109:1–4

But I am a man of prayer.
Psalm 109:4 (NIV)

When I first stumbled upon this passage it was almost shocking to me. At the time I was very concerned about a friend's situation. I was praying earnestly for my friend and to be honest, I found myself wondering just how effective prayer really was in situations like my friend's. And then I read this.

What makes today's quoted verse so remarkable are the verses that precede it. Though David did not write all the psalms, he was probably the writer of this one. In the first few verses of this psalm he writes some awful and even scary things. He says wicked and deceitful men have told lies about him. They have surrounded him with words of hatred. They fought against him without cause. In return for his friendship they accused him. Then he writes, 'but I am a man of prayer'.

David could have fought against these men. He was a mighty warrior. He could have judged them because he was the king. But what did he choose to do instead? He prayed. David, the soldier and king, considered prayer his best defence against these enemies. What a powerful model for us to live by!

Prayer: *Dear heavenly Father, thank you so much for the privilege of prayer. Regardless of our circumstances, help us to be people of prayer. In your Son's name. Amen*

Thought for the day: When we are troubled, prayer is our best choice.

Harriet Michael (Kentucky, US)

PRAYER FOCUS: MY ENEMIES

THURSDAY 20 NOVEMBER

Whose Way?

Read Isaiah 55:6–11

Jesus said, 'This is my commandment: love each other just as I have loved you.'
John 15:12 (CEB)

Twice I dreamed that I was driving on a two-lane road and a car appeared in my lane, coming from the opposite direction. I glanced at the other lane and saw another car moving in the same direction as I was. I was driving in the wrong lane.

When I awoke, I thought about my dreams. I recalled that when I drove in Jordan for the first time, even though I knew cars drive on the right side of the road, I failed to do so. When I drove up a slope to a traffic light, I faced many cars in front of me, waiting for the traffic light to change and heading in the opposite direction. I was stunned, and I quickly turned around.

Finally, I understood my dreams. Reading Isaiah 55:6–11, that day's Bible reading in *The Upper Room*, I thought about my recent struggles in faith. God's way is different from mine. I want to follow the commandment in John 15:12, but I easily slip back into old familiar ways. God helps me return to the right way. The more I struggle to get closer to him, the more I focus on the words of scripture. The word of God is holy promise: 'Love each other, just as I have loved you' (John 15:12). 'If you remain in me and my words remain in you, ask for whatever you want and it will be done for you' (John 15:7).

Prayer: *Loving God, thank you for your care and guidance. Keep us open to your promises and obedient to your commandment. In Jesus' name, we pray. Amen*

Thought for the day: Focusing on scripture draws us closer to God.

Kazumi Munehiro (Fukuoka, Japan)

PRAYER FOCUS: INTERNATIONAL TRAVELLERS

FRIDAY 21 NOVEMBER

A Better Future

Read Isaiah 43:15–21

The Lord says, 'Do not remember the former things, or consider the things of old. I am about to do a new thing; now it springs forth, do you not perceive it? I will make a way in the wilderness and rivers in the desert.'
Isaiah 43:18–19 (NRSV)

While on a cruise on the Yangtze river in China, we were instructed to look for old shoes floating by. Our guide explained that when people suffer illness, unemployment or divorce they let go of the past and its painful memories by putting their old shoes in the river. With new shoes they hope to walk into a better future.

In Isaiah 43:18, the Lord encouraged a sad and exiled people to let go of the grief of the past and instead to trust his leadership to enter a new place. With God's help, we can be refreshed. When I struggled with painful feelings of rejection after my divorce, I didn't understand how the Lord could bring anything good out of it. But this verse gave me courage to believe that God would lead me to a better life. As I did my best to trust and obey, our Lord brought me fresh joy and new purpose. God asks us to learn from our failures and mistakes but not to live in our past pain.

In Romans 6:4 Paul wrote, 'We have been buried with him by baptism into death, so that, just as Christ was raised from the dead by the glory of the Father, so we too might walk in newness of life.' We take steps toward newness of life as we daily turn from the temptation of despair and put our hope in God.

Prayer: *Dear Lord, who makes all things new, help us to let go of past defeat and guilt. In the light of your forgiveness and leadership, may we follow you into a future of hope. Amen*

Thought for the day: Jesus can make all things new (see Revelation 21:5).

Clifford B. Rawley (Missouri, US)

PRAYER FOCUS: THOSE STRUGGLING THROUGH A DIVORCE

SATURDAY 22 NOVEMBER

Spiritual Growth

Read Hebrews 5:7–14

I fed you with milk, not solid food, for you were not ready for solid food. Even now you are still not ready.
1 Corinthians 3:2 (NRSV)

In my student days I was addressed as 'Didi' (which means 'elder sister') by the children and teenagers in the neighbourhood. Several years later I became known as 'Aunty', which means an older person, like a mother. I did not like being addressed that way because it reminded me that I was ageing. Still a few years later, I moved to another state where I was even called 'Granny' by a few children. Soon I discovered that in that part of the state girls were given in marriage in their teens and became grandparents in their early forties. So I accepted the new name gracefully—though it took time. My image in the eyes of others changed with the passage of time, which took no extra effort on my part.

But achieving spiritual maturity requires our effort and intention. Born into God's family, we begin to grow spiritually when we hunger for his word, meditate on it regularly and apply it in our lives. The pure milk and then the solid food of the word of God help us to grow from infancy to childhood, then on to adulthood, and finally into mature Christians. In each step of the way we can become more and more like Jesus.

Prayer: *O God, we want to grow in our faith and in the likeness of Jesus. Help us, we pray. Amen*

Thought for the day: How is my spiritual growth evident to those around me?

Pramila Barkataki (Uttar Pradesh, India)

SUNDAY 23 NOVEMBER

Forever New

Read 2 Timothy 3:10–17

All scripture is inspired by God and is useful for teaching, for reproof, for correction, and for training in righteousness, so that everyone who belongs to God may be proficient, equipped for every good work.
2 Timothy 3:16–17 (NRSV)

I have a Bible on my e-reader. However, it seems ironic to be reading this sacred book that is 2000 to 3000 years old on such a device.

This reminds me of all the permutations these ancient words have gone through. The Bible contains 66 books—written on parchment or papyrus in Hebrew, Greek and Aramaic—by many different authors in different times and situations.

Even so, the Bible's road to the 21st century has been rough. God's word has been suppressed, hidden, opposed and sometimes even burned, but it has also been treasured and translated often. Here it is for anyone to read: the truth of God that leads us to grace, truth, love and peace.

Someday my e-reader will be as obsolete as the horse and cart, and what will take its place is anybody's guess. But even then, God's word of the truth and grace that we see in Jesus will be as fresh and contemporary as it is now.

Prayer: *Holy One, we are grateful for your living word that shines through every age. May your truth find a home in our hearts. This we pray in Jesus' name. Amen*

Thought for the day: The truth of God's word is eternal.

Philip A. Rice (Michigan, US)

PRAYER FOCUS: BIBLE TRANSLATORS

MONDAY 24 NOVEMBER

New Possibilities

Read Romans 11:7–16

I am speaking to you Gentiles. Inasmuch then as I am an apostle to the Gentiles, I glorify my ministry.
Romans 11:13 (NRSV)

Recently I was preparing for a very important trip and meeting with international partners. The meeting had been planned for several months, but sudden changes in the weather altered all our plans. Flights were cancelled, and it became clear that the meeting would not be taking place on the intended dates. I was upset. But later in the day my irritation left me when I realised that the postponement of the trip would allow me to spend more time with my family. I saw this as a gift and rejoiced in the opportunity.

The apostle Paul also found a way to make the most out of a changed situation. He faced many obstacles when he began to preach the gospel to Israel. His own people rejected the good news about Jesus. But this did not stop Paul. He did not lose hope that Israel would turn to God; in fact, he saw a new opportunity—to preach the gospel to the Gentiles. At that time this was a revolutionary idea. He saw himself as an apostle to the Gentiles. As we know, this attitude changed the world and the whole map of the Christian world. The entire then-known world heard the good news about Jesus Christ.

Prayer: *Great God, help us to see the opportunities in obstacles. Lead us by your Holy Spirit that we might act boldly like the apostle Paul. Amen*

Thought for the day: What opportunities to share the gospel can I find in today's obstacles?

Eduard Khegay (Moscow, Russia)

TUESDAY 25 NOVEMBER

Thanking God

Read 1 Timothy 6:6–8
I have learned the secret of being content in any and every situation.
Philippians 4:11 (NIV)

After Christmas, holiday literature drops through the letterbox, trying to persuade us that there is somewhere better that we ought to be, where the sea is bluer, beaches whiter, sunshine warmer, where we will be happier than we have ever been…

Every morning I thank God for my home and the place in which I live. It is so easy to be blind to the daily gifts we are given; most of us have food, warmth and home comforts.

The other day my friend and I tramped along the beach with my ecstatic dog who chased a ball, romping in the wet sand. Briefly we stopped. 'We are so lucky to be living in a place like this,' my friend remarked. I had to agree. The sea was reflecting a sky of pale turquoise and the sand was soft and fine. The air smelled of salt and seaweed and though the tide was out a rim of waves broke beyond the rocks. It seemed like Paradise, and again I thanked God.

Being satisfied is an art. After years of packing and lugging suitcases to distant parts, I feel I don't want to chase daydreams anymore. God has placed where he wants me to be, and my heart is full of gratitude.

Prayer: *Lord, thank you for all the gifts you give us each day. Help us to learn the art of being satisfied. Amen*

Thought for the day: Where the Lord is, there shall my heart be.

Pauline Pullan (North Yorkshire, England)

PRAYER FOCUS: PEOPLE WHO FEEL DISSATISFIED WITH LIFE

WEDNESDAY 26 NOVEMBER

Healing Touch

Read Matthew 9:18–26

[Jesus] said, 'Take heart… your faith has made you well.'
Matthew 9:22 (NRSV)

Several years ago I became ill and doctors told me they could treat my symptoms but that my condition would probably never go away. Dealing with my situation became the focus of my life as I searched for relief. Eventually, I became discouraged and turned to my Bible for solace. I began to look for biblical stories of illness and healing. One of the stories I read was of the woman who believed she could be healed if she could only touch Jesus' garment. Her belief was so strong that it led her to pursue Jesus so she could touch his clothing. When she did, Jesus told her that her faith had healed her.

Using this story from Matthew as a model, I began to pray for my healing, pursuing Jesus in prayer as I visualised myself touching the hem of his garment and my body being healed. I was not instantly healed; however, over time my attitude toward my situation changed. I stopped focusing on myself and started asking Jesus to use me as a vessel for his work.

Eventually my symptoms became more manageable, and today they are gone. Doctors say that someone with the health condition I had can experience spontaneous healing, but I will always believe that my healing came from the Lord.

Prayer: *Dear God, thank you for the Bible to guide us and inspire us. Amen*

Thought for the day: What Bible stories have helped you through a difficult time?

Vicki Hines (Tennessee, US)

THURSDAY 27 NOVEMBER

A Great Day!

Read Psalm 34:1–11, 17–20
When the righteous cry for help, the Lord hears, and rescues them from all their troubles.
Psalm 34:17 (NRSV)

Boyce, a friend who was single and a teacher, was facing a Christmas alone—his family was 2500 miles away—so we invited him to celebrate the day with our family. Within minutes of arriving, he was playing with the children, laughing, rolling on the floor and having a wonderful time.

The following spring, Boyce began to struggle with pronouncing words; he had to concentrate intently to complete a sentence. Soon after, he was diagnosed with Motor Neurone Disease. His condition deteriorated rapidly, but he continued to communicate via email. I vividly remember the way his last email began: 'I'm having a great day. I hope you are.' He described his physical condition: he no longer could walk or talk. He could barely raise one finger to slowly and meticulously type that email. Yet Boyce was having a great day.

I've noticed that Boyce and other Christians, who seem to be bubbling over with joy and contentment, and have a passion for life, all share an unwavering faith in our Lord and Saviour, Jesus Christ. The joy we seek is available through faith.

Prayer: *Almighty God, help us to understand that joy, contentment and peace are available to us through faith in you. Amen*

Thought for the day: Our joy is in the Lord.

Jeff Jenkins (North Carolina, US)

PRAYER FOCUS: PEOPLE SUFFERING FROM MND

FRIDAY 28 NOVEMBER

Our Personal Best

Read Philippians 3:10–14

Jesus said, 'I am the vine; you are the branches. If you remain in me and I in you, you will bear much fruit; apart from me you can do nothing.'
John 15:5 (NIV)

I enjoy watching track and field events. Especially exciting for me are the races: the tension of waiting for the starting gun, the sight of each runner straining to win, with their whole focus on the finish line. It is satisfying to cheer for the winners as they stand to receive their awards. We also cheer for the athletes who record a personal best time, even if they did not win. We celebrate with them as they realise they have done better than ever before.

Similarly, in our Christian discipleship, we can aspire to serve God more fully each day. As we live in fellowship with our Lord, we can strive to make each day our personal best for him. After all, Jesus speaks of our living in him, becoming branches of his vine, drawing nourishment from him and producing lasting fruit (John 15:5). We can bring all our energies to bear as we run toward the goal of becoming truly one with Jesus.

Prayer: *Gracious God, help us this day to do our very best for you. Amen*

Thought for the day: Today I will give my personal best for God.

Bill Willis (New South Wales, Australia)

PRAYER FOCUS: COMPETITIVE RUNNERS

SATURDAY 29 NOVEMBER

Willingness to Serve

Read Matthew 25:31–40

The king will say to those on his right, '… I was hungry and you gave me something to eat, I was thirsty and you gave me something to drink, I was a stranger and you invited me in.'
Matthew 25:34–35 (NIV)

A friend had promised to join me at the airport to offer company and assistance while I was travelling. When I arrived, my friend was not at the airport, and I was unable to reach him. I had no money to buy a meal, no phone and no internet access to send an email; so I sat, feeling lonely and afraid, as I waited for my flight. When a young man passed by, holding a mobile phone, I asked him to help me send a text message. Not only did he let me make a call, but he also bought me snacks for breakfast. How did he know I was hungry?

I am grateful to God for coming to me through a stranger, who met my needs and offered me comfort. This stranger's generous help reminded me of Matthew 25:40: 'Whatever you did for one of the least of these brothers and sisters of mine, you did for me.' I have learned to be vigilant, willing to offer assistance to someone in need, without prompting, because in so doing, I am serving the Lord.

Prayer: *Thank you, dear God, for your abundant and loving care. Give us a discerning spirit and willingness to assist those in need. In Jesus' name we pray. Amen*

Thought for the day: What opportunities are available for me to minister to the people I encounter today?

Philip Polo (Nairobi, Kenya)

PRAYER FOCUS: PEOPLE WHO ARE TRAVELLING

SUNDAY 30 NOVEMBER

A Clean Slate

Read Jeremiah 31:31–34

The Lord says, 'I will forgive their iniquity, and remember their sin no more.'
Jeremiah 31:34 (NRSV)

The children leaned forward to see what the minister was doing as he spoke of God's forgiveness. He wrote several words on a pad of paper. 'Oops!' he said, 'I've made a mistake.' Then he turned the pencil over and rubbed out the mistakes. 'That's what God does when he forgives us,' he said. 'God rubs out our mistakes, our sins, completely, as if they had never happened.'

As I watched, I realised that God does more. He forgives and does not remember our sins, as if the paper were restored to its original state. No sign of pencil marks remain. God gives us a clean slate.

In Jeremiah 31:31–34, the people of Israel were promised a new day, a new covenant, even though they had disappointed God over and over again. The promise now extends to all who believe in the new covenant established by Jesus Christ. 'If we confess our sins, he who is faithful and just will forgive us our sins and cleanse us from all unrighteousness' (1 John 1:9). We are forgiven.

Prayer: *Dear God, teach us to forgive as you forgive and to pray as Jesus taught us, 'Father, hallowed be your name, your kingdom come. Give us each day our daily bread. Forgive us our sins, for we also forgive everyone who sins against us. And lead us not into temptation.'* Amen*

Thought for the day: God erases our sins and gives us a clean page to begin anew.

Emily M. Akin (Tennessee, US)

PRAYER FOCUS: CHILDREN'S MINISTERS
* Luke 11:2–4 (NIV)

MONDAY 1 DECEMBER

The Chipped Cup

Read Exodus 4:10–12

We have gifts that differ according to the grace given to us.
Romans 12:6 (NRSV)

Recently my wife and I were sorting through some old dishes to decide which were suitable to give away and which were unsalvageable. At one point, when I rescued a cup that had a large chip in the rim, she looked surprised. 'It's my favourite cup,' I told her. 'It reminds me that we can be flawed but still useful.'

Throughout history, God has used people who were less than perfect. Moses was 'slow of speech and tongue' (Exodus 4:10, NIV). Rahab was a prostitute. David committed adultery with Bathsheba, and then arranged to have her husband killed in battle. Peter denied Jesus three times.

I also have many weaknesses and imperfections, and as I near retirement I am beginning to feel my age. My eyesight, hearing and memory aren't what they used to be, and the aches and pains are growing more frequent. But that doesn't mean I can't be useful. I can go into an uncertain future with confidence in my ability to keep serving the Lord because I know that he will be there with me.

Prayer: *Dear Lord, remind us that we can be useful in serving you despite our flaws. Amen*

Thought for the day: We don't have to be perfect to be useful to God.

Peter J. van der Linden (Iowa, US)

PRAYER FOCUS: PEOPLE NEARING RETIREMENT

TUESDAY 2 DECEMBER

Welcome Back!

Read Lamentations 3:22–26

The Lord said to Jacob, 'I am with you now, I will protect you everywhere you go.'
Genesis 28:15 (CEB)

Recently my wife and I travelled overseas for our first holiday in a decade. Not wanting to take my heavy Bible, I purchased a small New Testament, with Psalms and Proverbs. I also packed my copy of *The Upper Room* for our visit, fully intending to continue my devotional reading each day.

Although it was a wonderful trip, we had only seven days away; everything seemed rushed. When I met my two brothers for the first time in 32 years and visited my old homes on the other side of the world, I never made the time to read my Bible or the meditations at all. But my intentions had been good!

What a delight it was to return home to Australia and to catch up on two or three daily meditations each day, plunging myself back into the word of God! I became re-inspired. I also realised that God always waits for us to return, no matter how near or far we travel, or for whatever reasons we neglect to spend time with him. Always patient and welcoming, God rejoices in our presence.

Prayer: *Dear God, thank you for your constant presence in our lives. Forgive us when we distance ourselves from you. In Jesus' name we pray. Amen*

Thought for the day: God is always ready to welcome us back.

John Porter (New South Wales, Australia)

PRAYER FOCUS: FAMILY MEMBERS WHO ARE BEING REUNITED

WEDNESDAY 3 DECEMBER

Let it Go!

Read Psalm 138:1–8

The steadfast love of the Lord never ceases, his mercies never come to an end; they are new every morning; great is your faithfulness.
Lamentations 3:22–23 (NRSV)

Whatever I do, I try to do as unto the Lord. Other people say I am a perfectionist, but my results are not perfect—not at all! When the day comes to an end, I often feel frustrated or discouraged. I may feel so miserable and inadequate in my efforts to keep up with daily demands and challenges that I cry out to God. Then I let my imperfections go, and he gives me a sense of peace. How differently I perceive life when a new day comes and I open my heart before the Lord with thanksgiving and praise! Then I see God's faithfulness everywhere.

Jeremiah also lamented tragedies and trials in his life and in the life of God's people. Nonetheless, he said, 'This I call to mind, and therefore I have hope: The steadfast love of the Lord never ceases, his mercies never come to an end; they are new every morning' (Lamentations 3:21–23).

Each day, we remember that our perfection does not make life wonderful and our circumstances do not make life pleasant, but God's grace and mercy penetrate every aspect of our lives to make our days worth living.

Prayer: *Dear Lord, thank you for your love and mercy that sustain us from day to day. In Jesus' name, we pray. Amen*

Thought for the day: 'Whatever you do, work at it with all your heart, as working for the Lord' (Colossians 3:23, NIV).

Yulia Bagwell (Pennsylvania, US)

PRAYER FOCUS: PERFECTIONISTS

THURSDAY 4 DECEMBER

Opportunity

Read 1 Corinthians 1:26–31

Consider your own call, brothers and sisters: not many of you were wise by human standards, not many were powerful, not many were of noble birth.
1 Corinthians 1:26 (NRSV)

Our church in Bulgaria lives on the margins of society, despite the fact that our church buildings in the larger cities are often situated near the busiest city centres. Because of our church locations, to many it would appear that we must be one of the more influential mainline Christian denominations in our country. But the reality is completely different. We are a minority church with seemingly little influence.

For some this seems like a discouraging situation. But in fact, this is our chance to focus our attention beyond our own existence and survival. Our downtown churches are very close to the poor and marginalised in our local communities. We can understand their despair, pain and fear of being social outcasts. We can be faithful in sharing the good news among the people who need it most—the poor, the orphaned, the sick and those with addictions.

We discover our true call to ministry when we look beyond our church walls and the labels we Christians give one another. Then we have a great opportunity to welcome those who have no power—those who feel weak and alone—into the Body of Christ.

Prayer: *Dear God, give us loving hearts to serve others. Amen*

Thought for the day: The closer we are to people in need, the closer we are to God.

Daniel Topalski (Ruse, Bulgaria)

FRIDAY 5 DECEMBER

Cast out Fear

Read Psalm 40:1–5

Moses said to Joshua, 'It is the Lord who goes before you. He will be with you; he will not fail you or forsake you. Do not fear or be dismayed.'
Deuteronomy 31:8 (NRSV)

On the news I saw that the storm damage was horrific. Reporters interviewed residents who were not yet allowed to return home to see what damage their homes might have suffered. Victims wondered if their houses were still standing. If they were, how much damage would they have to deal with? How would they face the future?

Fear of the future can include so many different forms: job insecurity, fear for a loved one's safety, financial challenges and medical crises—to name a few. This is my personal fear of the future: in the next day or two, I will find out the results of a mammogram. My mother died of breast cancer, so I'm at increased risk. I'm usually able to give my cancer fears to God, but since the mammogram, the worried thoughts have multiplied and wreaked havoc with my imagination. Like a flood, the thoughts have been overwhelming me and I have felt as if I were drowning.

But in the midst of this anxiety, Bible verses reassure me that the God who has always stood by me in the past is with me today and is already in my future. I realise that ugly and difficult things may lie ahead, so I strive to have faith. I know that I can trust God no matter what I face.

Prayer: *Loving Father, help us to remember that you are with us in all circumstances. Cast out our fear of the future. Amen*

Thought for the day: With God beside me, I can be fearless.

Deb Vellines (Illinois, US)

PRAYER FOCUS: BREAST CANCER PATIENTS

SATURDAY 6 DECEMBER

Free Gift

Read Ephesians 2:1–9
It is by grace you have been saved, through faith—and this is not from yourselves, it is the gift of God.
Ephesians 2:8 (NIV)

I carefully reviewed my Christmas gift-and-card list, hoping that I hadn't missed anyone. I know how awkward I feel when someone gives me a gift and I don't have anything to give in return. I admit that I also dash off a last-minute card when I receive one in the post from someone who isn't on my list.

Even when someone does me a favour I find myself saying, 'I owe you one.' To be on the receiving end of a generous gesture without reciprocating is not in my nature.

Maybe that's why I need to remind myself, especially during the Christmas season, that God's most precious gift, Jesus Christ, was given out of the depth of God's love for us, not because we've earned it and certainly not because we deserve it. God loves us so much that he wants to be reconciled with us through the gift of Jesus Christ. God's unique gift is ours to accept with an open and grateful heart.

Prayer: *Dear heavenly God, help us humbly to receive the gift of your Son, Jesus, and to keep gratitude in our hearts all year long. Amen*

Thought for the day: God's love is the greatest gift of all.

Kay L. Campbell (Connecticut, US)

PRAYER FOCUS: THOSE WHO HAVEN'T ACCEPTED THE GIFT OF GOD'S SON

SUNDAY 7 DECEMBER

Press On to the Goal

Read Philippians 3:10–14

I press on to take hold of that for which Christ Jesus took hold of me.
Philippians 3:12 (NIV)

We watched Andy Murray, the British tennis player, leave the court. He was not happy. He would receive a large sum of money and great acclaim for reaching the semi-final of the Wimbledon tournament, but he was not satisfied—he had lost to another great player. 'I must train harder,' he said to the listening crowd. 'Next year I'll be back!' Winning at that level means complete dedication; treating the game as a hobby is not enough, neither is talent alone. The player must go all out to win. And the following year, Andy Murray achieved his elusive goal of winning Wimbledon.

God is always more willing to give than I am to receive. We would think that the apostle Paul was doing well in his Christian life, but he wanted *everything* that God had prepared for him. He was not about to sit back and feel that he had everything God was going to give him. He did not treat his faith like a hobby, but as a goal he wanted to go all out to reach.

Prayer: *Thank you, Lord, that there is so much that you want me to have. Like Paul, I intend to press on and take hold of everything you have prepared for me. Amen*

Thought for the day: Will I settle for less than God wants me to have?

Marion Turnbull (Liverpool, England)

PRAYER FOCUS: FOR A PASSION FOR GOD IN OUR CHURCH LIFE

MONDAY 8 DECEMBER

Remembering the Good

Read Psalm 105:1–6

O give thanks to the Lord, call on his name, make known his deeds among the peoples.
Psalm 105:1 (NRSV)

Some years ago, when our son was suffering from depression, our family slipped into a dark place. It was difficult to see the light, helpfulness and generosity of others. We were seeking God, but our situation did not seem to be getting better.

During one family counselling session, however, the counsellor asked us to list our blessings, to evaluate the good things in our lives. We noted the blessings of our faith, the kindnesses others had shown to us and the fact that our family was still whole and intact.

In time, a spirit of thanksgiving returned. We discovered new ways to talk to each other and also found that God was never far away. Being thankful can transform us. As the psalmist noted centuries ago, when we are thankful, we are proclaiming God's works—and others can also remember what the Lord has done for them.

Prayer: *Generous God, help us to be thankful for our blessings, especially when life is difficult. In this way we are witnesses to your love. Amen*

Thought for the day: A spirit of thanksgiving brings us closer to God.

Todd Outcalt (Indiana, US)

PRAYER FOCUS: THOSE WHO SUFFER FROM DEPRESSION

TUESDAY 9 DECEMBER

Seasons

Read Ecclesiastes 3:1–14

For everything there is a season, and a time for every matter under heaven.
Ecclesiastes 3:1 (NRSV)

For over ten years I've endured a chronic health disorder, but thankfully I'm able to function for the most part. My most difficult times bring about painful digestive problems. During my peaceful seasons, though, I feel much better and so thankful to God for this time of mercy flowing over me.

Over time I have grown to appreciate all the changing seasons of my health. Through God's love I was finally able to see that if I could identify the seasons of my pain, then I could see how God was not only keeping me but helping me to find a deeper gratefulness in the quieter times.

One of my favourite Bible verses is Ecclesiastes 3:1. This verse affirms that in every aspect of our lives and every stage of life, we are forever moving through seasons in some way. The good news is that with God's strength we can learn not only to accept the challenges but humbly to appreciate those highs that will help us to endure our lows.

Prayer: *Dear Lord, help us to see your healing hands and loving arms holding us during our times of pain. Amen*

Thought for the day: How is God present for me in this season?

Sharon Owens-Davis (New Jersey, US)

PRAYER FOCUS: THOSE WHO LIVE WITH CHRONIC ILLNESS

WEDNESDAY 10 DECEMBER

Playing with Passion

Read 1 Corinthians 12:4–20
In Christ we, though many, form one body, and each member belongs to all the others. We have different gifts, according to the grace given to each of us.
Romans 12:5–6 (NIV)

At a recent Christmas concert, I noticed again the way the elements of a musical programme work together. The players of each musical instrument, singers of each choral part, soloists and conductor all had a place and a purpose. Some elements were more prominent than others but all were essential. And together they sounded phenomenal.

Someone could have said, 'The sheet music contains every note of every piece. So why play it? Why sing it? We know what it sounds like and how it will progress and end.' But knowing how it will sound or how it will end is not the point. The point is to experience it. We came to be caught up in the wonder of beautiful music passionately rendered.

Each of us has a place in God's grand symphony—of his kingdom come, his will be done on earth as it is in heaven. We each have a part to play. Some parts are more prominent than others but all are essential. Just knowing about God or how to live our lives is not the point. Shouldn't we rather be caught up in the wonder of lives passionately lived?

Prayer: *Dear God, thank you for the blessing of our Christian family and the opportunity to serve you together. Amen*

Thought for the day: What part has God given me to play in this symphony of life?

Peter N. Lundell (California, US)

THURSDAY 11 DECEMBER

God's Choice

Read 1 Samuel 16:1–13

The Lord does not see as mortals see; they look on the outward appearance, but the Lord looks on the heart.
1 Samuel 16:7 (NRSV)

The Lord had rejected Saul as king of the Israelites and sent Samuel to the little-known family of Jesse to choose a new king. Jesse's sons were called into the presence of the Lord, but none was chosen. Jesse's youngest son, David, was a shepherd out tending his father's sheep. Jesse never thought of bringing him into the presence of the Lord, thinking he was not a suitable candidate. But when David was presented to Samuel, the Lord approved and he was anointed king.

God's choices are not determined by family background, physical appearance, social status, political strength or majority vote. David lacked many of the prerequisite qualities in human eyes, but he was the right candidate in God's eyes.

My call to ministry was similar to David's call. Nothing worth mentioning distinguished my family, compared to families in my clan that were known for flourishing businesses, educated individuals and respected farmers. But from my little family, the Lord chose me to be a shepherd of the church. Just as God called me, he calls each of us to service in this world.

Prayer: *Dear God, help us to understand that we are chosen despite the shortcomings other people see in us. Amen*

Thought for the day: God still chooses unlikely people to serve the world.

T. Ruwodo (Harare, Zimbabwe)

PRAYER FOCUS: CHURCH LEADERS

FRIDAY 12 DECEMBER

Best Gift

Read Psalm 3:1–5

In peace I will lie down and sleep, for you alone, Lord, make me dwell in safety.
Psalm 4:8 (NIV)

My mother was always a generous gift-giver during her life. But one of the most meaningful gifts I ever received from her came after her death at the age of 88. While I was sorting through her belongings, a sheet of her personalised stationery slowly drifted to the floor. I realised that it was handwritten Bible verses from her favourite book, Psalms. Her handwriting had become almost illegible, but to my surprise this was written in a strong, confident hand. During those years of declining mental and physical health, she had found solace in the beautiful poetry and prayers from Psalms 3 and 4. I imagined her carefully writing out words that gave her comfort—words that would now give me comfort in the difficult days and nights following her death.

I framed this declaration of my mother's faith and placed it on my desk in my home office. It reminds me every day of God's assurance that we can 'lie down in peace and sleep' as he watches over us. When fear and worry rob us of the sleep our body requires, we can 'call out to the Lord' and he will give us the rest we need.

More precious than any present purchased at a shop is God's promise that we can feel safe and secure in loving arms.

Prayer: *Loving Father, keep us under your graceful watch today and give us a peaceful rest tonight. Amen*

Thought for the day: God's faithfulness is a treasured gift.

Sarah M. DuBose (South Carolina, US)

PRAYER FOCUS: THOSE WHO HAVE DIFFICULTY SLEEPING

SATURDAY 13 DECEMBER

The Healing Power of Prayer

Read Psalm 92:1–5
It is good to give thanks to the Lord, to sing praises to your name, O Most High.
Psalm 92:1 (NRSV)

It was just after our grandson's christening when our son phoned us to let us know that his partner had been airlifted to hospital following the rupture of a cerebral aneurysm, complicated by heart failure and subsequent cardiac arrest. She was put into an induced coma and attached to equipment to provide circulation, but was given less than ten per cent chance of survival. Our whole family was devastated and we felt so helpless. We prayed for her recovery and that her brain should not be damaged since there was a high risk of it.

We shared her condition with our church family and asked friends in other churches to pray for her too. We later discovered that many Christians we did not know were also praying.

Over several weeks she began to improve and was taken out of her coma, and though she needed more operations over many months she gradually got better. She has no brain damage apart from slight memory loss.

It has been a year since this happened, and we still thank God for his wonderful love, miraculous healing power and care through the doctors and nursing staff. We also witnessed the powerful effect of the prayer of many Christians in different parts of the world, and thank God for them.

Prayer: *Lord, we thank you for your compassion and love for us, and we pray that you may use us in your service. Amen*

Thought for the day: May we praise and glorify God every day.

Eileen Griffiths (Ross-shire, Scotland)

PRAYER FOCUS: THOSE WHO ARE ILL WHO NEED OUR PRAYERS TODAY

SUNDAY 14 DECEMBER

God's Great Love

Read Luke 18:15–17
God's love was revealed among us in this way: God sent his only Son into the world that we might live through him.
1 John 4:9 (NRSV)

As jubilation for the Christmas season increases, I am reminiscing about my early years at school. We sang about the sweet story of old, when Jesus lived here among us and loved little children, calling them lambs of his fold. Singing those hymns often brought me close to him. And now I feel mesmerised all over again as I recall my desire to have Jesus' hands placed on my head in blessing and his arms around my shoulders in loving embrace.

Even now Jesus is mine. The more I acknowledge his companionship with me, the more fellowship I have with him every day. He is my friend.

Therefore, despite the turmoil and turbulence in the world, I remember that Christmas, celebrating the birth of Christ, is meant to be the sweetest, brightest and most joyous season because God showered love on earth. I pause and pray, welcoming Christ once again.

Prayer: *Thank you, God, for your great love in giving your son Jesus to be born among us. Amen*

Thought for the day: Jesus Christ is 'love divine, all loves excelling, joy of heaven, to earth come down' (Charles Wesley, 1747).

Zaina Renner (Western Province, Sierra Leone)

PRAYER FOCUS: FOR THE WORLD TO KNOW GOD'S BOUNDLESS LOVE

MONDAY 15 DECEMBER

Trusting in the Lord

Read Psalm 37:3–6

Trust in the Lord with all your heart, and lean not on your own understanding; in all your ways submit to him, and he will make your paths straight.
Proverbs 3:5–6 (NIV)

My young grandson loves playing and swimming in the pool. When he was barely two years old, I watched as he walked out on to the diving board, ready to jump into the water. Being the ever-cautious grandfather, I was very scared for him. He looked down and said, 'My daddy catch me.' What trust he put in his dad as he leaped into the deep section of the pool! He was absolutely certain his dad would reach out and catch him when he hit the water after jumping off the diving board.

I will never forget his words. Would that we could put that much faith and trust in our heavenly 'daddy'! Jesus directed us to consider the example of children. We adults often fear situations that might overwhelm us. But if we hold fast to God's hand, knowing that our heavenly Father loves us, we have no reason to fear.

Prayer: *Dear heavenly Father, we thank you for your love and care. Help us to put our trust in you in every situation and to know that you are there to catch us when we fall. Amen*

Thought for the day: God is our ever-present help in every situation.

John Allen Berry (Tennessee, US)

PRAYER FOCUS: GRANDPARENTS

TUESDAY 16 DECEMBER

An Infinite Love

Read Psalm 23:1–6

We know that all things work together for good for those who love God.
Romans 8:28 (NRSV)

I saw Lia for the last time last summer at the seaside. Her face was pale and strained with suffering. Her eyes, though circled with dark rings, were still luminous and lively even though she was thin from chemotherapy. Lia was bursting with love from every pore, and she lavished it on those around her. It was lovely to see her play happily with her grandchildren. When I lost the companion of my life, Lia and her family had offered me their loving support. 'I shall always be here for you,' she said to me, enveloping me in her warm hug, although it was she who needed help.

'The Lord is my shepherd, I shall not want.' Lia fully understood this verse and made it her own message of hope. She trusted in God's merciful love and gave generously of herself without becoming discouraged in the difficult times. Lia's body was frail but her indomitable spirit never faltered. She was sustained by her faith in the prospect of salvation offered by God in Christ, who, by his sacrifice on the cross, has vanquished death and given us eternal life in his kingdom.

Prayer: *Lord, give us the strength to alleviate sorrow through solidarity with our neighbour. Amen*

Thought for the day: Christ's love overcomes the barrier of death.

Elisabetta Pagano (Campania, Italy)

PRAYER FOCUS: FAMILIES OF CANCER PATIENTS

WEDNESDAY 17 DECEMBER

A Christmas Gift of Thanks

Read Galatians 6:8–10
Whenever we have an opportunity, let us work for the good of all.
Galatians 6:10 (NRSV)

When one of our church members was collecting money for the Salvation Army at the supermarket, a homeless man approached him and noticed the sign stating that the collectors were from our church. The homeless man asked, 'What church is that?' The church member pointed toward our building down the street. The homeless man pulled a few coins from his pocket, dropped them into the collecting tin and said, 'They've been good to me.'

That man's gift to the Salvation Army was also a beautiful gift to each of us who share in the mission of making God's love real through our church. He spoke for people whose names we will never know and whose faces we may never see, who would speak the same words of gratitude for this church and its ministries in our city and around the world.

God's love that became flesh in Jesus continues to become flesh whenever any of us help those in need with our prayers, presence, gifts and service.

Prayer: *Dear God, may we never grow weary in showing your love to others through our words and deeds. As Jesus taught us, we pray, 'Our Father in heaven, hallowed be your name, your kingdom come, your will be done, on earth as it is in heaven. Give us today our daily bread. And forgive us our debts, as we also have forgiven our debtors. And lead us not into temptation, but deliver us from the evil one.'* Amen*

Thought for the day: Jesus becomes flesh in us when we help those in need.

James A. Harnish (Florida, US)

PRAYER FOCUS: LOCAL COMMUNITY OUTREACH
* Matthew 6:9–13 (NIV)

THURSDAY 18 DECEMBER

Loving Doubting Thomas

Read John 20:24–29

Now faith is the assurance of things hoped for, the conviction of things not seen… By faith we understand that the worlds were prepared by the word of God, so that what is seen was made from things that are not visible.
Hebrews 11:1, 3 (NRSV)

As a child, I found faith in God easy. I felt it when singing hymns and hearing Bible stories in Sunday school and church. I felt it when I prayed. As I got older, though, I found that holding on to my faith—and even, sometimes, a belief in God—was difficult. I remembered the story of 'Doubting Thomas'. Thomas was not one of the first witnesses to Jesus' resurrection, but Jesus appeared to him a week later and told him, 'Do not doubt but believe' (John 20:27). I found parallels between my own struggles and those that Thomas went through.

I have sympathy for Thomas. I take heart that Jesus understood there would be doubt among his followers. After years of feeling lost, I take comfort in God. I view my struggles with faith, not as failures but as opportunities to seek Jesus and to look for the signs of him in my daily life. I find relief, knowing that he loves me and forgives me. He is with me to show me his wounds and to heal mine.

Prayer: *Dear God, help us to use our doubt as an opportunity to seek your word and to strengthen our love, life and faith. Amen*

Thought for the day: Our doubts and struggles can strengthen our faith and commitment.

Karyn Schumpert (Colorado, US)

PRAYER FOCUS: THOSE WHO ARE STRUGGLING WITH DOUBT

FRIDAY 19 DECEMBER

Elephants and Crickets

Read Psalm 1:1–3

Whatever is true, whatever is noble, whatever is right, whatever is pure, whatever is lovely, whatever is admirable—if anything is excellent or praiseworthy—think about such things.
Philippians 4:8 (NIV)

Have you ever had an elephant in your house? Probably not! But if you ever did, you would know exactly where it was. Have you ever had a cricket in your house? Last year I did, and I spent days searching for it. I would listen for that high-pitched chirping, and just when I thought I had found it, the chirping would stop. I spent a lot of time on this little cricket—looking for it, listening for it. But when I stopped focusing on the cricket, one day it left my house.

At times life brings us 'elephants': the huge ordeals of death, divorce or disease. But for the most part, our days are spent with the crickets: those little things in life that seem to annoy us, stress us, dominate our thoughts and take our minds off more important things.

When our days seem full of cricket chatter, we can intentionally tune it out by turning to the Lord through scripture and prayer. We can think about whatever is just, whatever is pure, whatever is commendable and worthy of praise. When we are listening for God's word, we won't be able to hear the crickets!

Prayer: *Gracious God, keep our thoughts on you today and how you want to use us in your world. In Jesus' name. Amen*

Thought for the day: When I'm thinking about God, I won't hear the crickets.

Michael Vaughn (Tennessee, US)

PRAYER FOCUS: THOSE STRUGGLING TO HEAR GOD

SATURDAY 20 DECEMBER

Tempted

Read James 1:12–18
Blessed is anyone who endures temptation.
James 1:12 (NRSV)

The supermarket aisles were jammed with Christmas shoppers, and customers jostled to the tills. A store employee helped me to unload my shopping trolley. As the total came up on the till screen and I reached for my purse, I noticed a black plastic square at the bottom of my trolley. I didn't remember that being there before. I was being hurried along when I realised that the black square was an upturned tray of very expensive steak. *You're going to hold everyone up. Think of the savings! No one will know. It's not your fault.* Amid all these thoughts, I had to make an instant decision about whether to give in to this temptation or do the honest thing.

'I'm sorry but something has been missed.' My bill was adjusted, and I left. As I walked away from the mutterings and sighs of impatient customers, I also was aware of an incredible sense of peace.

Our lives are filled with major temptations. However, Christ can give us the strength to triumph, even in the little ones.

Prayer: *Dear Lord, keep our hearts pure before you. In the little temptations as well as major choices, be our guide and strength this day. In Jesus' name we pray. Amen*

Thought for the day: God will see and know the choices we make.

Faye Roots (Queensland, Australia)

SUNDAY 21 DECEMBER

Songs of the Great Reversal

Read 1 Samuel 2:1–10

[The Lord] seats [the poor] with princes and has them inherit a throne of honour.
1 Samuel 2:8 (NIV)

Three songs that are recorded in the Bible tell of God's great reversals. Hannah rejoiced, liberated from her barrenness. Moses and Miriam led the singing when the Israelites escaped from Egypt (Exodus 15:20–21). Mary, the mother of Jesus, celebrated the deliverance her son would bring (Luke 1:46–55).

From these songs, we can learn much about God's nature and will for us. Hannah sang about God's exalting the poor, whom we regard as helpless and unworthy of honour. We find new purpose as we learn to value people who are not considered important.

Moses saw the great reversal in the way the Lord leads with love (Exodus 15:13). No longer was power found in brute strength, but in the love of God. We find new purpose in discovering that no good comes from violence and retaliation, but only from love.

Mary described the great reversal in terms of God's mercy (Luke 1:50). God exalts the lowly, who recognise their need for God. Our purpose does not depend on our own power, but on the strength of love, which comes from the Lord and in community with one another.

Prayer: *Dear Lord, attune our lives to your great reversal, established in your grace and justice. Amen*

Thought for the day: What is the theme of my song of praise to God today?

Eleanor Shepherd (Quebec, Canada)

PRAYER FOCUS: FEMALE CLERGY

MONDAY 22 DECEMBER

Outward Appearance

Read James 2:1–5

Peter began to speak to them: 'I truly understand that God shows no partiality.'
Acts 10:34 (NRSV)

When I entered the shop, he caught my attention immediately. The young man came from a race different from mine. He had an unusual haircut and was dressed in a manner that I considered offensive. He looked out of place.

After shopping, I went to the self-service till to pay for my groceries. Fumbling with the items and my wallet, I scanned and paid for them. As I walked out of the store, I felt a tap on my shoulder. I turned around to see the young man I had noticed earlier. He handed me my wallet. I had not realised that I had dropped it.

As much as I was relieved to have my wallet returned, I was ashamed at how I had 'profiled' this young man. As a teacher, I have worked successfully with students of many races and nationalities. I should have known better than to make assumptions about someone based on their race and appearance. Thankfully, God does not judge us by our appearance. I relearned a valuable lesson that day about not judging people by the way they look.

Prayer: *Holy God, help us to see the best in everyone and to look beyond outward appearances. Amen*

Thought for the day: God sees what is inside each of us.

Tim Wood (Tennessee, US)

TUESDAY 23 DECEMBER

Not Guilty

Read John 3:16–17
The wages of sin is death, but the free gift of God is eternal life in Jesus Christ our Lord.
Romans 6:23 (NRSV)

In *Mesto Vstrechi* (the Russian edition of *The Upper Room*), I met a sister from New Mexico who encouraged us to pray for 'complacent church members'. I began to think about each of our church members to sort out the complacent ones. For some reason, I could think of no one. But surely there must be someone? Again I considered everyone in my church, and since I could think of no one else, I decided that I must be the guilty one.

This is a continual struggle for me—to accuse myself of everything bad. I could not escape from this habit even when I discovered salvation in the Lord. I know that the Lord died a painful death to save people from the burden of guilt and sin. But still I struggled with self-accusation.

Probably others have the same problem. But each of us can receive freedom from guilt when we are able fully to accept and believe the word of the Lord. I am grateful to this sister from New Mexico and to the staff of *Mesto Vstrechi*. They have helped me today to hear the Lord bless me with words that give me peace and make me feel grateful: 'I love you so much that I have sent my son to take away your sins and guilt' (see John 3:16).

Prayer: *Dear Lord, help us to trust your promises so that we might feel the fullness of your joy. Amen*

Thought for the day: Christ offers forgiveness. Do I accept it?

Roza Tyu (Moscow, Russia)

PRAYER FOCUS: THOSE WEIGHED DOWN BY GUILT

WEDNESDAY 24 DECEMBER

Christmas Eve

Read Luke 2:41–52

[Jesus] said to [his parents], 'Why were you searching for me? Did you not know that I must be in my Father's house?'
Luke 2:49 (NRSV)

I am a father of eight children in a blended family. My wife and I both serve as step-parents to children from previous marriages. Being a step-parent is often a tough and thankless job. We have both heard words like: 'You're not my dad' or 'I don't have to listen to you.' While blended-family dynamics are often difficult, our family has strengthened over time as we face and overcome obstacles. Knowing that God's grace is greater than divorce and brokenness, we keep Christ at the centre of our family.

Realising that God through Christ Jesus chose to enter a human family gives us hope. In today's reading, Luke's Gospel shares a very human situation from Jesus' childhood. Mary and Joseph lost Jesus in Jerusalem. After searching for three days they found him not at home but in the temple. I can imagine Joseph's feelings when Jesus tells them 'Did you not know that I must be in my Father's house?'

This story reminds me that God is the Father of us all. The good news is that Christ experienced a human life, a human family and a human death to pay the penalty for our sins. Through Christ's sacrifice we are all one blended family, and we too can claim God as our Father.

Prayer: *Dear heavenly Father, we thank you that through Christ we are all one family. Amen*

Thought for the day: We are all children of God.

Michael Beck (Florida, US)

THURSDAY 25 DECEMBER

Christmas Day

Read Colossians 3:15–17

In Christ Jesus you are all children of God through faith.
Galatians 3:26 (NRSV)

Every Christmas season one of my responsibilities as musical director is to prepare a cantata with my church choir for our congregation. This year we also presented the cantata at a local nursing home and invited the residents to join us in singing familiar carols. No lyrics were provided for this special performance, but when I gave the signal for the audience to join in, the residents—even those with dementia—sang with all their hearts. They needed no help in recalling the carols they loved so much. Those words of God's love were etched into their memories, and nothing could prevent the words from bubbling up from deep within.

As we sang of shepherds, wise men and angels, we saw that although we had obvious physical differences, the residents and choir members merely belonged to separate generations of God's family. They, the older brothers and sisters and we, the younger, were all simply children of God, saved by grace. In that glorious moment of singing together, God allowed me a glimpse of a time when his entire family will sing for ever in the presence of our Saviour. And what a choir that will be! Hallelujah! Glory to the newborn King!

Prayer: *Thank you, Lord, for loving us so much. Help us to look beyond our physical differences and realise that we all belong to you. Amen*

Thought for the day: God's children come in all shapes and sizes—and ages.

Jacob C. Schneider (Maryland, US)

PRAYER FOCUS: NURSING HOME RESIDENTS

FRIDAY 26 DECEMBER

Only Temporary

Read Matthew 6:19–33

We fix our eyes not on what is seen, but on what is unseen, since what is seen is temporary, but what is unseen is eternal.
2 Corinthians 4:18 (NIV)

While putting the Christmas ornaments away, I discovered that one of them—a handcrafted treasure commemorating our oldest child's first Christmas—was beginning to disintegrate. Made of highly varnished bread dough, it had lasted almost 30 years. 'I suppose I should have known this one would be temporary,' I said and then realised that all the ornaments are temporary.

Ephemeral, inanimate belongings make up such a large part of daily life. Increasing numbers of us, it seems, have difficulty letting go of them. When we are faced with the agonizing need to dispose of a few cherished school drawings or sports trophies, it helps to remember that absolutely none of our material possessions will last for ever.

Often it is not the items themselves but what they represent that I prize. As I learn to relinquish my grip on material things in favour of the intangible values they represent, I find the blessings of God's presence each day.

Though bittersweet, letting go of things offers the grace of deepened wisdom as we learn to move forward in life, relying only on God's eternal presence.

Prayer: *Dear God, help us to let go of temporary things and focus on what will last—the truth you offer us in Jesus. Amen*

Thought for the day: Material possessions will pass away, but God's love and truth will endure.

Julia Denton (Virginia, US)

PRAYER FOCUS: THOSE TRYING TO SIMPLIFY THEIR LIVES

SATURDAY 27 DECEMBER

Unexpected Blessing

Read Psalm 121:1–8

Where does my help come from? My help comes from the Lord, the Maker of heaven and earth.
Psalm 121:1–2 (NIV)

I enjoy running. One Saturday morning, I was hoping to do some training on a nearby hill. But it was already humid and the hot sun blazed down from a clear blue sky. Both these factors reduced my chances to train very well.

But when I came to my training hill, something above the road caught my attention. While I had seen the row of green-leafed tall trees along the street, I had not noticed the way they arched over the road, blocking the hot sun. While the humidity was still in the air, the unexpected shade allowed me to have a safe and productive workout.

When I realised what the shade of the trees provided to help me, the verses from Psalm 121 came to mind, 'The Lord is your shade at your right hand; the sun will not harm you by day' (vv. 5–6). I found myself feeling very thankful for the unexpected and personal way I had experienced God's blessing that day.

Prayer: *Dear God, thank you for the unexpected surprises of your overarching grace and love in our lives. Amen*

Thought for the day: Today, I will watch for signs of God's personal love for me.

Doug Wilson (New York, US)

PRAYER FOCUS: RUNNERS AND WALKERS

SUNDAY 28 DECEMBER

Moments with God

Read Colossians 1:3–12

Pray continually, give thanks in all circumstances; for this is God's will for you in Christ Jesus.
1 Thessalonians 5:17–18 (NIV)

Every Sunday during our church service, we invite anyone who has had an inspiring experience with God during the week to tell the congregation about it. One Sunday, a woman who had volunteered to weed our church flowerbed told us how she watched people as they walked past our town-centre church. She said she wondered about each person—what they did, if they were happy or troubled, what their life story was. Then she offered a brief prayer for those she saw, asking God to bless them, to ease their burdens and to grant them peace.

Recently I had been feeling that my prayer life was in a rut, praying over and over for the same friends, family members and concerns. Inspired by this woman's prayer practice, I decided to pray every morning and night for a week for a specific person, whether or not I knew him or her. It might be a visitor to my church, someone I read about in the newspaper or someone who caught my attention while I went about my day.

I hope that those for whom I pray feel God's presence in their lives. I know that praying for someone who will never know of my prayers surely brings God's joy to me!

Prayer: *Dear heavenly Father, bless those we pass by as we go about our lives. Tend to their needs and give them your peace. In Jesus' name. Amen*

Thought for the day: Asking God's blessing for someone else also blesses us.

Susan Griswold (Colorado, US)

PRAYER FOCUS: FRIENDS AND STRANGERS WHO CROSS OUR PATH

MONDAY 29 DECEMBER

God's Unfailing Strength

Read Isaiah 41:8–10

Don't fear, because I am with you; don't be afraid, for I am your God. I will strengthen you, I will surely help you; I will hold you with my righteous strong hand.

Isaiah 41:10 (CEB)

I felt the helicopter lift off the pad. I was strapped on to a narrow stretcher, struggling to breathe through an oxygen mask. An emergency paramedic watched me carefully. 'Are you OK?' she asked.

I nodded, but I wasn't OK. The A&E doctor had ordered that I be flown to a big-city hospital. I knew I was in danger of dying. 'Is this it?' I asked God.

'No, this isn't it,' came God's strong, certain reply.

I settled back and peered through the window at the white clouds and blue sky. My anxiety subsided. I felt a quiet strength flood my being. I knew I was going to be all right, no matter what.

Isaiah reminds us that God chose a tiny, ragged band of people to be God's own. In doing so, he promised to hold them and to sustain them through all their trials. They were not always faithful to God and not always grateful, but he was always with them. His powerful love would not let them go. The promises belong to us, too. God's nature is to love and strengthen us through all the difficult times in our lives.

Prayer: *Loving God, thank you for sustaining us through all the trials in our lives. Remind us that you are always close, and help us to be faithful. Amen*

Thought for the day: God is the source of our strength.

Denise Kirk-Hall (Texas, US)

PRAYER FOCUS: EMERGENCY MEDICAL TEAMS

TUESDAY 30 DECEMBER

Our Anchor

Read Hebrews 6:13–20

We have this hope as an anchor for the soul, firm and secure.
Hebrews 6:19 (NIV)

It was a glorious day, and we were in our boat at the mouth of the river. My husband was engrossed in fishing, and I was focused on reading my book. Suddenly someone called out, alerting us that we had lost our anchor. Not only had we drifted dangerously close to the other boat, but my husband could no longer keep fishing without our anchor. So we headed for shore.

This experience reminded me of the truth that Jesus is our anchor. He is our lifeline and our hope. When he is our centre, the one we rely on, he keeps us steady and productive. On the other hand, if we take our eyes off Jesus and become involved in our own agendas, then without even knowing it, we can find ourselves drifting away from the love and grace he offers.

That day I remembered the words of Hebrews 6 and the confidence I have because Christ is the steadfast anchor in my life.

Prayer: *Thank you, Father, for giving us Jesus as our anchor and our hope. As he taught us, we pray, 'Our Father which art in heaven, Hallowed be thy name. Thy kingdom come. Thy will be done in earth, as it is in heaven. Give us this day our daily bread. And forgive us our debts, as we forgive our debtors. And lead us not into temptation, but deliver us from evil: For thine is the kingdom, and the power, and the glory, for ever.'* Amen*

Thought for the day: Christ is reliable on glorious days and in storms.

Ann Stewart (South Australia, Australia)

PRAYER FOCUS: ANGLERS
* Matthew 6:9–13 (KJV)

WEDNESDAY 31 DECEMBER

The Man Who Was Willing

Read 2 Corinthians 9:6–12

God loves a cheerful giver.
2 Corinthians 9:7 (NRSV)

Excited to have a free hour to relax, I settled into my favourite chair with all my quilting materials within reach. A few minutes later the doorbell rang. Grudgingly, I headed for the door, followed by my nine-year-old daughter, Emily. In the cold, driving rain stood a man with no coat or umbrella, holding a clipboard. After greeting us, he went on to explain that he was collecting money for a church mission programme. Preoccupied by my desire to return to my quilting, I responded with a polite but short, 'I'm sorry, but I can't help you today' and slowly closed the door.

Emily asked, 'Why? Why did we give nothing? He came out in the cold and rain to collect money for the poor.' Instantly, my heart sank. The honest answer was that my self-centredness had caused me to miss this opportunity to help someone, as well as the chance to teach my daughter about how God loves a cheerful giver.

A short time later, Emily handed me a drawing entitled 'The man who was willing'. She had expressed on paper what was in her heart. On this day, my young daughter was the teacher. Her childhood artwork remains both a treasured keepsake and a valuable lesson. Fifteen years later, Emily still draws when her heart is profoundly touched, and I strive not to miss any opportunity God gives me to be a cheerful giver.

Prayer: *Dear God, help us to be generous and truly willing to help others in need. Amen*

Thought for the day: In spite of our mistakes, God gives second chances.

Kathleen Hoover (California, US)

PRAYER FOCUS: THOSE WHO SERVE THE POOR

Small Group Questions

Wednesday 3 September

1. Describe a time when you failed. How did you feel? How did you know you had failed? Who knew about your failure?

2. Do you have knowledge about or experience of any kind of abuse? What would you want to tell someone who is experiencing abuse? What resources, comfort or help can you or others offer to people in abusive situations?

3. How does your church community talk about or acknowledge abuse in the community or in the world? What scriptures, spiritual practices or ministries could be offered to help those who are experiencing or are recovering from situations of abuse?

4. Grace describes hearing the Holy Spirit assure her in her darkest moment. How has the Holy Spirit spoken to you? How do you make time to listen for the Holy Spirit in your life?

5. When have you been most aware of and thankful for God's abundant grace? Describe that experience and how you felt when God's grace surrounded you.

Wednesday 10 September

1. How can you relate to today's meditation? Do you identify with Julie's experience or the experience of her parents? What personal experience helps you to empathise with this story?

2. Who do you know who is feeling overwhelmed by the responsibilities of caring? How can you reach out to them to offer support or help?

3. Relationships change over time. How has your relationship with God changed throughout your life? How has your prayer life changed? How do you hope it will be different in the future?

4. What spiritual practices help you to treasure your time with God? Describe a particular place or experience that helps you feel close to him.

5. How does your church community offer support to ageing members and the people who care for them? How could these ministries be expanded or revitalised?

Wednesday 17 September

1. Ellen tells us that Guillermo noticed and complimented her the first time she wore make-up. Recall a time when someone noticed something about you and complimented you. Were you surprised by their attention? How did the compliment make you feel? Why do you still remember that moment?

2. How has your life or the life of someone you know been shaped by violence? How does violence affect your daily life? Your community? Your country?

3. Recall a time when you received tragic news. How did this news affect your faith? Did you question God at that moment?

4. Read Ephesians 4:11–13. Who in your life has inspired you to live a life of faith? What spiritual gifts did that person have? How did that person build up the body of Christ in his or her life?

5. Ellen states: 'Guillermo is more alive now than he ever was on this earth.' How do you react to this statement? Have you ever felt a similar way toward someone whom you've lost?

Wednesday 24 September

1. What Bible verses or stories give you hope and encouragement? When have these verses or stories been particularly helpful or meaningful to you?

2. Camille describes her grandmother as an 'amazing woman of faith'. Describe an amazing woman of faith that you have known. How did she shape or inspire your faith?

3. How have you learned about the Bible over the course of your life? What classes, practices, studies or conversations have helped you to explore the Bible more deeply? How have you shared your knowledge with others?

4. In 2 Timothy 1:5, Paul implies that children 'inherit' the faith of their parents. How much influence do you think that parents, grandparents and other family members have on the children in their family?

5. What physical reminders of God's presence would someone find in your home? How big a part do these play in your daily life?

Wednesday 1 October

1. If you heard someone with a life-threatening illness say, 'It is better this way', how would you react? What would you say to that person? What questions would you want to ask?

2. When have you prayed for God to remove an obstacle from your path? What was that obstacle, and what was God's response to your prayer? How did this experience affect your faith in God?

3. When someone you know is struggling with a serious illness, how do you show your love and support? How could you help others reach out to people in your community or church who are ill or struggling?

4. Read Psalm 51:10 aloud. What would it mean to you to have a new and right spirit? How would this change the way you interact with people? How would it change the way you live?

5. Have you ever drawn the conclusion that God's power was made perfect in your weakness? What experience(s) led you to that conclusion?

6. Verner's friend Abe has gone on to live a long and full life. Would your response to this meditation have been different if we had been told that Abe died a year after his diagnosis? Why or why not?

Wednesday 8 October

1. Mark was reminded of the daily sins in his life by the dirt on his glasses. When have you had an experience that reminded you of your daily sins? How did that experience change your daily spiritual practice?

2. What sins do you most easily become accustomed to and overlook? What helps you to be mindful of these 'little' sins? How do you work to avoid these sins?

3. What does the word 'sin' mean to you? How would you describe sin to someone who is unfamiliar with the term? Why is it important to know what sin is? How does sin affect your relationship with God?

4. How does your church talk about sin? In what contexts do you discuss sin? How do your church leaders encourage you to deal with sin and feelings of guilt?

5. Read 1 Peter 2:24. How does knowing that Jesus died for your sins affect your faith and your daily life? How do you strive to 'live for righteousness' in your daily living?

Wednesday 15 October

1. Recall a time when you felt frustrated or irritated during worship. What contributed to your frustration? What did you do about it? How did this affect your worship experience that day?

2. When you are worshipping, are you mostly focused on the people in the building and what is happening around you, or are you focused on the people in the world beyond your church building? Do you think one of these points of focus is better than the other? Why or why not?

3. What does the celebration of Communion mean to you? Is it a meaningful part of your faith practice? How does this ritual connect you more closely with God? How does it connect you more closely to the people in your church or around the world?

4. Through the incarnation, God became human in the person of Jesus Christ. How does knowing Jesus lived a human life shape the way you communicate with God?

Wednesday 22 October

1. Do you remember when you became a Christian, or have you always been a believer? What has been the most formative moment of your faith journey so far? What moment in your faith experience do you most want to share with others?

2. Have you ever been told how a Christian should behave? What are some of the words used to describe a good Christian? What passages of scripture do people use to define good Christian behaviour? How are these words helpful or restrictive to you?

3. God's people are diverse. How do you view diversity? Does interacting with people who are different from you make you nervous? Excited? Curious? Describe a time when you interacted with someone very different from you. What did you learn? What surprised you?

4. What part of your physical body or personality have you struggled to accept? Why? How has your faith helped or made it difficult for you to learn to love yourself? Who has helped you to realise that you are a beloved child of God?

Wednesday 29 October

1. Have you or someone you love struggled with addiction? What was most difficult about that experience? What kind of help and support did you or your loved one most need?

2. How has your faith been strengthened or challenged by difficult circumstances? How has prayer helped you during these times? What have you learned about yourself or your faith through these struggles?

3. In Exodus 17:12, Aaron and Hur held up Moses' hands to support him and help their people. When have you supported someone in a difficult time? What did you do? What kind of support was most appreciated or helpful? What kind of support was easiest or hardest for you to offer? Why?

4. When have you felt most welcomed and supported by a community? Describe the community. How did they welcome you? In what ways did they support you?

5. In 2 Corinthians 1:3–7, Paul addresses believers who are experiencing the same sufferings that he and Timothy are suffering and states that they can share with others the comfort that God gives. Do you think it is easier or harder to comfort someone who is struggling with a problem you have struggled with before? Why or why not?

Wednesday 5 November

1. How do you relate to Shadia's experience in this meditation? Do you agree or disagree with her understanding of leading and dominance? What personal experiences have shaped your understanding of what it means to be led or dominated?

2. Describe a time when, through a new experience, your perspective changed. How did this experience feel? Were you uncomfortable? Relieved? How did this experience affect your faith or your relationship with God?

3. Who comes to mind when you think about good leadership? What are the qualities of a good leader? What problems arise with poor leadership?

4. How have you learned to trust God? What experiences of faith have helped you to know God as a good leader?

5. How would you help someone who has not yet learned to trust God's leading? What practices or experiences would you encourage them to seek?

Wednesday 12 November

1. Do you enjoy giving gifts? Do you know someone like Heidi's friend who loves to give thoughtful, extravagant gifts? How do you feel about giving or receiving extravagant gifts?

2. Describe a time when you received an unexpected gift that you were not prepared to reciprocate. Did you feel guilty? What did you do?

3. Gracious receiving can be just as important and meaningful as gracious giving. Do you know someone who is a gracious receiver? How does it feel to give that person a gift? What does the gracious receiver do or say to let you know that the gift is appreciated?

4. Heidi describes her realisation that wanting to repay God for the gift of salvation is not the point of the gift. How do you resonate with Heidi's feelings of guilt, indebtedness and gratitude toward God?

5. The next time you receive a gift, how will you respond?

Wednesday 19 November

1. Harriet writes that reading this passage was 'almost shocking' to her. What Bible passages have shocked you? When you are shocked or surprised by scripture, how do you react? What do you do to better understand that passage?

2. When have you doubted the power of prayer? What circumstances or experiences have shaped your understanding of prayer and its effectiveness?

3. Can you relate more easily to Harriet's reaction to Psalm 109:1–4 or to David's decision to pray?

4. Who has modelled a life of prayer for you? What about that person do you admire or respect? If you were to ask them why they pray, what do you think they would say?

5. How does your church community instruct and encourage people to pray? How does prayer fit into the ministry and life of your church?

Wednesday 26 November

1. Have you or has someone you love received a discouraging diagnosis? How did you react to the news? Where did you turn for support and healing?

2. What Bible passages have helped you through difficult times? How did reading and reflecting on these passages help you persevere or trust God more deeply?

3. There are many stories of healing in the Bible. What story is your favourite or the most powerful for you? Why?

4. Imagine that you are the woman in Matthew 9 who needs healing. From what do you need to be healed? How do you want Jesus' power to act in you? Visualise yourself touching the hem of Jesus' garment. What would healing feel like for you? How will you continue to pray for healing this week?

Wednesday 3 December

1. Yulia describes her struggle with perfectionism. Is this a struggle for you? If not, what struggles cause you to lament or feel inadequate? How do you deal with your struggle? Where do you turn for help and support as you seek to love yourself and your life in spite of your struggles?

2. Prayer is a way of turning worries, fears and struggles over to God. Describe a time when you were able to give your worries to him. How did that feel? Were you able to sense his peace in that moment?

3. Where do you see God's love and faithfulness in your life? In your community? In your church? How do you acknowledge or celebrate God's presence with you each day?

4. What do you need to release to God today? What practices or prayers can you use to help you?

Wednesday 10 December

1. Recall a time when you witnessed or participated in good teamwork. How did people determine who would perform what role? What made the team successful?

2. In I Corinthians 12:4 Paul writes that 'there are different kinds of gifts, but the same Spirit distributes them' (NIV). Name some spiritual gifts and describe people who display those particular gifts. What are some of your spiritual gifts?

3. How does your church help people identify and use their spiritual gifts? What study groups, tools or ministries does your church offer that help people develop spiritual gifts?

4. The Thought for the Day asks, 'What part has God given me to play in this symphony of life?' How do you answer that question? What is God calling you to do or be in this time of your life? How are you working to discern your part in serving God?

Wednesday 17 December

1. Read Mark 12:41–44. What parallels do you see between this Bible story and the encounter described in today's meditation? What do you think is the important lesson to be learned from the widow and the homeless man?

2. Where have you seen God's love in action this week? Describe that experience. How have you shown God's love to another person recently?

3. How is your church connected to or involved in the life of your city or town? What ministries, services or other outreach opportunities help members of the church interact with members of the community? What is your church known for in your town?

4. What charities or ministries do you donate to during Advent and Christmas? What are the attributes of these organisations that encourage you to give? What are some ways you can give back to your community during this season?

Wednesday 24 December

1. How do you relate to Michael's description of family and parenting? What experiences or observations help you to identify with Michael or his children?

2. What does it mean to you that Christ chose to enter a human family? How does Jesus' experience of being part of a family help you to persevere when family relationships or friendships are difficult?

3. Michael describes the family of God as 'one blended family' with God as our Father. What are some of the challenges that come from being one big family of God? Name some of the challenges facing the Church and God's family today. How do you strive to love the members of God's family with whom you disagree?

4. What does it mean to you that you are a child of God? How do you explain or describe this to others? How does being a child of God affect the way you live your life?

Wednesday 31 December

1. Describe a time when a stranger asked you for money. How did you react? What did you say? Did you give any money? Did you give something else?

2. What causes you to miss opportunities to help others? What helps you to recognise opportunities to help when they arise? How do you make time to give and volunteer?

3. How does your church communicate the needs of members and of the community? How do people learn of ways they can help others? How might this process be improved?

4. Kathleen tells us that her daughter Emily 'draws when her heart is profoundly touched'. How do you respond when you experience God in profound ways? How can you encourage others to share their experiences with God?

Journal page

Journal page

Journal page

Journal page

Journal page

Journal page

Journal page

Journal page

Journal page

NEW FROM BRF

80 Creative Prayer Ideas

A resource for church and group use

Claire Daniel

Prayer is a vital part of the Christian life but people often struggle with actually getting on and doing it. This book offers 80 imaginative and creative ideas for setting up 'prayer stations', practical ways of praying that involve the senses— touching, tasting, smelling, seeing, and hearing, rather than simply reflecting—as we bring our hopes, fears, dreams and doubts to God.

Developed from material tried and tested with small groups, the ideas provide activities ranging from bubble prayers to clay pot prayers (via just about everything else in between), and have been designed to be used with grown-ups of all ages.

ISBN 978 1 84101 688 7 £8.99

To order a copy of this book, please turn to the order form on page 159.

NEW FROM BRF

Journalling the Bible

40 writing exercises

Corin Child

The spiritual discipline of journalling has become increasingly popular in recent years and this book shows how it can fruitfully overlap with creative writing to provide an original way of engaging with the Bible.

'Bible study' is usually taken to mean 'reading and discussing'—but writing offers a different way of interacting with the text, generating new insights and application even from the most familiar of passages. *Journalling the Bible* offers 40 writing/journalling exercises that have been tested in workshops around the country, providing an imaginative resource for individual and group work and a refreshingly different way to become better acquainted with scripture.

ISBN 978 1 84101 736 5   £7.99

To order a copy of this book, please turn to the order form on page 159.

NEW FROM BRF

Longing, Waiting, Believing

Reflections for Advent, Christmas and Epiphany

Rodney Holder

This book of daily Bible readings and reflective comment covers the weeks from 1 December through to Epiphany on 6 January. As well as considering the well-known events of the nativity story, it looks back to those who prepared the way—the patriarchs and prophets of the Old Testament and John the Baptist and Mary the mother of Jesus in the New Testament.

The book also explores the traditional Advent focus on the 'four last things': death, judgment, heaven and hell. Rodney Holder shows how these sombre themes have their place in the build-up to the celebrations, because of another historic aspect of Advent: reflecting on the second coming of Jesus, when he will return, as Lord and King rather than helpless baby, to set the world to rights.

ISBN 978 1 84101 756 3   £7.99
To order a copy of this book, please turn to the order form on page 159.

NEW FROM BRF

The Act of Prayer

Praying through the lectionary

John Birch

The Act of Prayer is a comprehensive volume of contemporary prayers based on themes arising from the Common Worship lectionary, the three-year cycle of Bible readings followed by many churches. Each set of prayers comprises an opening petition plus prayers of adoration, confession and thanksgiving for each of the Sundays in the church calendar plus extra festival days.

Designed to resource and inspire people leading prayer in church services, this imaginative book is particularly suitable for any who are taking first steps into this ministry, as well as those looking for original prayer material to use in small group settings.

ISBN 978 1 84101 619 1 £9.99

To order a copy of this book, please turn to the order form on page 159.

How to encourage Bible reading in your church

BRF has been helping individuals connect with the Bible for over 90 years. We want to support churches as they seek to encourage church members into regular Bible reading.

Order a Bible reading resources pack

This pack is designed to give your church the tools to publicise our Bible reading notes. It includes:

- Sample Bible reading notes for your congregation to try.
- Publicity resources, including a poster.
- A church magazine feature about Bible reading notes.

The pack is free, but we welcome a £5 donation to cover the cost of postage. If you require a pack to be sent outside the UK or require a specific number of sample Bible reading notes, please contact us for postage costs. More information about what the current pack contains is available on our website.

How to order and find out more
- Visit **www.biblereadingnotes.org.uk/for-churches/**
- Telephone BRF on 01865 319700 between 9.15 am and 5.30 pm.
- Write to us at BRF, 15 The Chambers, Vineyard, Abingdon, OX14 3FE.

Keep informed about our latest initiatives

We are continuing to develop resources to help churches encourage people into regular Bible reading, wherever they are on their journey. Join our email list at **www.biblereadingnotes.org.uk/helpingchurches/** to stay informed about the latest initiatives that your church could benefit from.

Introduce a friend to our notes

We can send information about our notes and current prices for you to pass on. Please contact us.

BRF is a Registered Charity

Subscriptions

The Upper Room is published in January, May and September.

Individual subscriptions

The subscription rate for orders for 4 or fewer copies includes postage and packing: THE UPPER ROOM annual individual subscription £15.00

Church subscriptions

Orders for 5 copies or more, sent to ONE address, are post free:
THE UPPER ROOM annual church subscription £11.85

Please do not send payment with order for a church subscription. We will send an invoice with your first order.

Please note that the annual billing period for church subscriptions runs from 1 May to 30 April.

Copies of the notes may also be obtained from Christian bookshops.

Single copies of The Upper Room will cost £3.95. Prices valid until 30 April 2015.

Giant print version

The Upper Room is available in giant print for the visually impaired, from:

Torch Trust for the Blind
Torch House
Torch Way,
Northampton Road
Market Harborough
LE16 9HL

Tel: 01858 438260
www.torchtrust.org

Individual Subscriptions

☐ I would like to take out a subscription myself (complete your name and address details only once)

☐ I would like to give a gift subscription (please complete both name and address sections below)

Your name...

Your address..

....Postcode..

Your telephone number..

Gift subscription name..

Gift subscription address..

....Postcode..

Gift message (20 words max)...

....

Please send *The Upper Room* beginning with the January 2015 / May 2015 / September 2015 issue: (delete as applicable)

THE UPPER ROOM ☐ £15.00

Please complete the payment details below and send, with appropriate payment, to: BRF, 15 The Chambers, Vineyard, Abingdon OX14 3FE

Total enclosed £ .... (cheques should be made payable to 'BRF')

Payment by ☐ cheque ☐ postal order ☐ Visa ☐ Mastercard ☐ Switch

Card no: ☐☐☐☐ ☐☐☐☐ ☐☐☐☐ ☐☐☐☐ ☐☐☐☐

Expires: ☐☐☐☐ Security code: ☐☐☐

Issue no (Switch): ☐☐☐☐

Signature (essential if paying by credit/Switch card) ....

☐ Please do not send me further information about BRF publications

☐ Please send me a Bible reading resources pack to encourage Bible reading in my church

BRF is a Registered Charity

Church Subscriptions

☐ Please send me ... copies of *The Upper Room* January 2015 / May 2015 / September 2015 issue (delete as applicable)

Name..

Address ....

....Postcode.....................................

Telephone ....

Email..

Please send this completed form to:
BRF, 15 The Chambers, Vineyard, Abingdon OX14 3FE

Please do not send payment with this order. We will send an invoice with your first order.

Christian bookshops: All good Christian bookshops stock BRF publications. For your nearest stockist, please contact BRF.

Telephone: The BRF office is open between 09.15 and 17.30. To place your order, telephone 01865 319700; fax 01865 319701.

Web: Visit www.brf.org.uk

☐ Please send me a Bible reading resources pack to encourage Bible reading in my church

BRF is a Registered Charity

ORDER FORM

REF	TITLE	PRICE	QTY	TOTAL
688 7	80 Creative Prayer Ideas	£8.99		
736 5	Journalling the Bible	£7.99		
756 3	Longing, Waiting, Believing	£7.99		
619 1	The Act of Prayer	£9.99		

POSTAGE AND PACKING CHARGES				
Order value	UK	Europe	Surface	Air Mail
Under £7.00	£1.25	£3.00	£3.50	£5.50
£7.00–£29.99	£2.25	£5.50	£6.50	£10.00
£30.00 and over	FREE	prices on request		

Postage and packing
Donation
TOTAL

Name _____ Account Number _____

Address _____

_____ Postcode _____

Telephone Number _____

Email _____

Payment by: ❏ Cheque ❏ Mastercard ❏ Visa ❏ Postal Order ❏ Maestro

Card no ☐☐☐☐ ☐☐☐☐ ☐☐☐☐ ☐☐☐☐ ☐☐☐

Valid from ☐☐☐☐ Expires ☐☐☐☐ Issue no. ☐☐☐

Security code* ☐☐☐ *Last 3 digits on the reverse of the card. ESSENTIAL IN ORDER TO PROCESS YOUR ORDER

Shaded boxes for Maestro use only

Signature _____ Date _____

All orders must be accompanied by the appropriate payment.

Please send your completed order form to:
BRF, 15 The Chambers, Vineyard, Abingdon OX14 3FE
Tel. 01865 319700 / Fax. 01865 319701 Email: enquiries@brf.org.uk

❏ Please send me further information about BRF publications.

Available from your local Christian bookshop.   BRF is a Registered Charity

About brf:

BRF is a registered charity and also a limited company, and has been in existence since 1922. Through all that we do—producing resources, providing training, working face-to-face with adults and children, and via the web—we work to resource individuals and church communities in their Christian discipleship through the Bible, prayer and worship.

Our Barnabas children's team works with primary schools and churches to help children under 11, and the adults who work with them, to explore Christianity creatively and to bring the Bible alive.

To find out more about BRF and its core activities and ministries, visit:

www.brf.org.uk
www.brfonline.org.uk
www.biblereadingnotes.org.uk
www.barnabasinschools.org.uk
www.barnabasinchurches.org.uk
www.faithinhomes.org.uk
www.messychurch.org.uk
www.foundations21.net

If you have any questions about BRF and our work, please email us at

enquiries@brf.org.uk